ML 20/24   TRA

To David wishing
happy Christmas and happy
Thoughts of the future.
            Sandra.   1967.

The Highlands

Looking from Ben Lui to Ben Cruachan, Argyllshire

THE
HIGHLANDS

Ian Finlay

B. T. BATSFORD LTD
London

First published 1963
Second impression 1966

© Ian Finlay, 1963

MADE AND PRINTED IN GREAT BRITAIN BY
WILLIAM CLOWES AND SONS LTD, LONDON AND BECCLES
for the publishers B. T. BATSFORD LTD
4 FITZHARDINGE STREET, PORTMAN SQUARE, LONDON W.1

CONTENTS

ACKNOWLEDGMENT

The Author and Publishers wish to thank the following for permission to reproduce the illustrations appearing in this book:

R. W. Baker, for fig. 16.
J. Allan Cash, for fig. 2.
Noel Habgood, for figs. 3, 4, 12, 14, 18, 27, 30–3 and 36.
David Innes, for fig. 11.
John Leng & Co. Ltd., for figs. 1, 15, 17, 20, 25, 29 and 37 (from photographs by Robert M. Adam).
Donald B. MacCulloch, for fig. 8.
Alasdair Alpin MacGregor, for fig. 6.
The Ministry of Works, for fig. 9 (Crown Copyright).
D. D. C. Pochin Mould, for fig. 7.
The Mustograph Agency, for fig. 10.
J. D. Rattar, for fig. 23.
Kenneth Scowen, for figs. 19 and 26.
Edwin Smith, for figs. 13, 21, 24, 28 and 34.
Fred G. Sykes, for fig. 35.
Valentine & Sons Ltd., for fig. 22.

The Author would also like to acknowledge the help given by his colleague Dr. Charles Waterston, who kindly read the proofs of the introductory chapter and made certain amendments in those sections describing the geology of the region.

LIST OF ILLUSTRATIONS

List of Illustrations

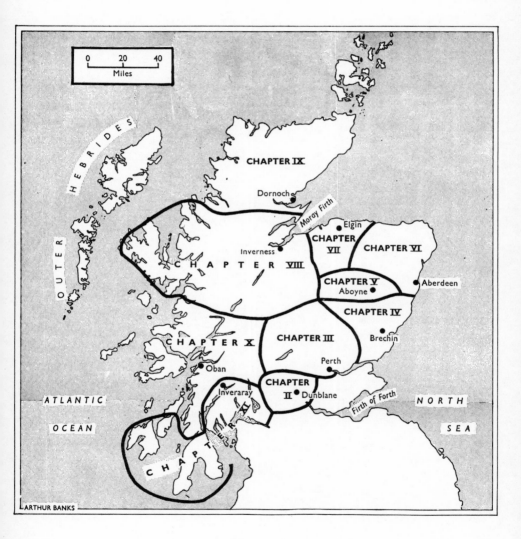

CHAPTER IX

Dornoch

Moray Firth

Elgin

Inverness

CHAPTER VII

CHAPTER VI

CHAPTER VIII

CHAPTER V

Aboyne

Aberdeen

CHAPTER IV

CHAPTER III

Brechin

CHAPTER X

Perth

Oban

CHAPTER II

Inveraray

Dunblane

Firth of Forth

CHAPTER I

HEBRIDES

OUTER

ATLANTIC

OCEAN

NORTH

SEA

0   20   40
Miles

ARTHUR BANKS

13

CHAPTER ONE

Introductory

From the battlements of Stirling Castle, it looks to be an easy matter to divide Scotland in two parts and to call them the Highlands and the Lowlands. Over there, beyond the flat carselands of the Forth, is what appears to be another country. Rank upon rank of mountain-tops fill the horizon from the hazy west to far in the north-east. Probably cloud-banks are lying on the peaks even if it is blue above the farm-lands about Stirling, so that over there in the north the skies themselves are different. Surely what lies beyond that mountain barrier is the Highlands, a self-contained region, geologically and ethnically and culturally quite different from the south?

In point of fact, no middle-European frontier problem is more difficult of solution than to draw a line between the Scottish Highlands and the Lowlands. A geographer might boldly draw it from somewhere back of Aberdeen to the south end of Loch Lomond and call all to the north of that the Highlands; but he knows that with the Laigh o' Moray, Caithness and some other localities he is including areas which are not Highland at all, while from a purely physical point of view in the Southern Highlands he is excluding a region in parts nearly as high and quite as wild as much of the far north. The anthropologist is in even more of a quandary. All are not Gaels to the north of the "Highland Line", while there are plenty of Gaels to the south of it, to say nothing of the Celtic stock of old Strathclyde. In writing this book, convenience would suggest following the practice of the Scottish rugby football authorities, who for reasons of their own call everything beyond the Antonine Wall the north of Scotland, but I cannot find it in me to embrace in the Highlands the Kingdom of Fife—even if

Macbeth, one of the earliest of all the Finlays, would not have hesitated to do so. My Highland Line, therefore, runs from the lower reaches of the Tay down to Cowal and Kintyre. However suspect it may be geographically and ethnically, this region has a certain completeness in atmosphere, in sentiment, for nearly all of it is within sight of the great Highland massif, is watered by its rivers, and within scent of its aromatic airs.

The Highlands as an entity are a creation not so much of the up-heavals of Nature as of the Victorians. Nature certainly erected a great range of primeval mountains there, but as usual she did her best to wear down and erode what she had heaved up. The legion commander look-ing out northwards from the parapet of Housesteads fort on the Great Whin Sill saw nothing between him and Ultima Thule but a single wilderness up out of which those peculiarly stubborn barbarians, the Painted Men, might at any moment come against him, threading the bogs and vaulting the streams on their spears. Agricola and others tried to seek them in their lairs, but they melted away, and what we know as the Highlands was simply the unprobed core of the wilderness. In subjugating this wilderness the earlier Stewart kings went much further than Agricola, and the Butcher Cumberland went further still; but none succeeded in the task as the Victorians succeeded. They did it by turning the whole mountainous area of central and northern Scotland into a sort of precursor of the national parks. Instead of proscribing the clans and their outlandish customs and costumes and weapons, as the Hanoverians did, only to drive those things underground, they fostered them. Following princely example, white-kneed stockbrokers from the City adopted the garb of the Gael, constructed new granite castles in the glens, built railways with machicolated turrets on their bridges. In short, they created a *mystique*. As with most *mystiques*, snobbery was a considerable element, and it became the thing to do to have a stake of some kind in clan territory.

This expensive playground had everything: magnificent scenery, excellent sport, a healthy climate, a background of history easily romanticised, a wonderfully polite peasantry. It was far enough away from the big centres of population to escape vulgarisation. It is true the Scotch middle classes also acquired the habit of going on Highland holidays, but they were not great in numbers and they seldom strayed far from the golf-courses which, by the end of Victoria's reign, had been laid out at many of the major resorts. In the end, indeed, the Scotch middle classes were an important part of the whole thing, for not only did they subsidise those golf-courses and encourage good hotels, but they provided an admiring and well-behaved audience and in many lesser ways helped to realise the dream of the Highlands as it had been so lovingly sketched by the Queen in the pages of her diary. In this age of bus-tours, beer bottles and banana-peel it is a little unfashionable to write tolerantly of Balmoralism, and in other books even I myself have tried to show something of the other side of the picture; but for many people it was a comfortable illusion while it lasted, nor was it in every sense an illusion either for, like the British Raj in India, it has left behind a certain strange, bitter-sweet nostalgia not among the departed sahibs alone.

Altogether it would have been easier to write this book in those days. Not only were there fewer doubts about the definition of the Highlands and the identity of the Highlanders: there were landmarks and reassuring rituals which progress has destroyed. It is too easy now to cross the Highland Line by car without being aware that anything of significance has happened. Even as recently as the 'twenties the train journey through Glenfarg was followed by a solemn ceremony in Perth station, when one changed to a green train with a foreign look and mingled on the platform with the Highland equivalent of those swarthy, mustachio'd figures who in the Gare de Lyons hang about the doors of coaches marvellously labelled Brindisi and Palermo. I recommend to the Scottish Tourist Board that they make it more and not less difficult to penetrate the Highlands, for what we come by too easily does not taste as sweet.

In wilder times the Highlands were indeed difficult to penetrate. That barrier effect as seen from Stirling is not an illusion, for the mountains and glens in the main strike south-west and north-east. The rocks of this region are some of the most ancient in the British Isles, relics of the process which geologists sometimes grandly call the Caledonian orogenesis, but man has had a foothold here for much less time than he has in the south, since the Highlands were in the main probably uninhabitable during the Glacial epochs. One feature of this massif must at once impress anyone looking at it from Stirling. Varied and tumbled as many of the peaks are, there are no groups which tower high above their fellows as there are in the Alps or the Himalayas. There is a levelling off or crushing down of the tops which seems to point to some factor limiting upthrust or somehow dictating uniformity. This is lost sight of when one gets among the hills, but when they are viewed in a broad sweep from a distance the absence of dominating peaks is marked. What one sees is the relics of a range which once may have rivalled any on earth. And worn stumps most of them look, rounded in outline, with only here and there the contrast of a dramatic peak where an iron-hard boss of quartzite is extruded, as in the cases of Schiehallion or Ben-y-ghlo, where metamorphic grits endure as Ben Ledi or Ben Vorlich, or where a sheer mass of granite rears up as it does in Ben Nevis itself. To the beginner few Highland mountains look difficult to climb. Only experience teaches of the treachery lurking in the traverse of some slimy "boiler-plate" or in the rotten rock of an ancient, frost-riven ridge. This and much trudging in boggy glens and through the driving mist on high moorlands may be needed to show why invaders found these modest mountains such formidable obstacles.

The second feature which generally marks the Highlands is the north-east to south-west "strike". On the map, it looks as though a rake had been drawn raggedly from the Moray Firth coast down towards the Irish Sea. The strongest evidence of this directional strike is presented by the great wall of the Highlands which we can see from Stirling, and by the Great Glen which, filled by Loch Ness, cuts the Highlands in two. Both are the result of gigantic faults in the rock formations. The first has been called one of the finest examples of a fault scarp to be found anywhere, towering as it does above a valley excavated in the belt of Old Red Sandstone stretching from Angus to the Clyde. Some suppose there has been a sideways thrust of the rock masses along the line of the Great Glen fault. Across the strike of those long ridges and valleys are a few less well-defined routes which penetrate the mountain system. The most prominent of them is the route which carries the Great North Road from Perth up over the Drumuachdar Pass, after which it follows the strike down the head-waters of the Spey, to deviate again at Carrbridge and carry the road across Slochd summit to Inverness.

The two great north-east to south-west faults and the penetration route of the Great North Road between them conveniently divide the Highlands into three regions. First, there is what may be called the Grampian region, comprising everything to the east of the Great North Road. Second, there is the west Highland region. This covers all the country west of the road and south of the Great Glen and its continuation in Loch Linnhe. Third and last, there is the North-west Highland region, from the Great Glen to Cape Wrath. These are not geological regions, although each has its well-marked geological features. A combination of geological and climatic factors, however, makes each distinctive as a region. Moreover, they are convenient divisions from the point of view of a visitor to the Highlands: a visitor who is more than a casual tourist, a visitor determined to get to know the Highlands, and one who likes to conduct his visit in a systematic way. He could spend, say, a month in each and build up impressions of the three regions, their scenery and atmosphere and the character of the people, which would fit together in a balanced picture of the Highlands as a whole.

In the Grampian region two basic geological elements seem to determine character and "feel": the Old Red Sandstone and the granite formations. The sandstone occurs principally between Perth and Stonehaven, revealing itself in the great red crag of Dunottar and in the brown rock of which Arbroath and other places in Angus are built. The Sidlaws and neighbouring hills that are outliers to the Grampians are the residue of volcanic activity during the laying down of the Lower Old Red Sandstone. The rich fruit-growing soils of the Carse of Gowrie and the farmlands of Angus are also products of the sandstone. The granites appear chiefly as mountain masses from the Cairngorms east to Lochnagar, and Aberdeen itself is built upon, and of, granite quarried from the immense pit of Rubislaw which is so large that, gazing into it, one loses all sense of scale. These mountains are not at first sight spectacular. They are so rounded by glacial action that they seem to have little height, and it is with astonishment that on a hot June day one notices from far off the snow-filled gullies on what appear to be gentle hills. With realisation, they suddenly acquire stature in every sense. Granite has also made the straths of Spey and Dee what they are, for they are floored with drifts of granite scree, providing perfect drainage, among the consequences of which is the finest heather in Scotland. It is a country of clear, fast-running streams, of pinewoods and purple moors, and in spite of the straths' mere few hundred feet of elevation the air is more subtly aromatic than in any Swiss mountain resort. Here, in winter and spring at least, latitude makes up for lack of altitude, and alpine conditions may be found at less than 1,000 feet above sea level. The Cairngorms themselves rise to well above 4,000 feet, and the Lochnagar massif to nearly as much, and these attract clouds and rain; but the straths, and still more the flat coastlands of the Moray Firth, are not wet. Indeed, the country about Elgin, Forres and Nairn is among the driest in the British Isles: the Garden of Scotland, it has been called, with its mountain-fed rivers sparkling seawards through its cornfields and plantations. Fertile too are the farmlands to the south of the Cairngorms and their foothills, from Strathmore eastwards to Montrose, but it is a heavier soil, and there are apt to be damp fogs coming in off the sea. This is the country from which J. M. Barrie escaped and which Lewis Grassic Gibbon remained in and immortalised, and is the only area embraced by this book which wholly resists inclusion in the Highlands.

The West Highland region is completely different from the Grampian. It contains some of the loveliest scenery in the world, and this is largely due to the circumstance that so much of its beauty is mirrored in water. It is a country of fjords, similar in many ways to the Westland region of Norway, and like Norway it has, in the Inner Hebrides, a protecting screen of islands which give it great tracts of calm coastal waters ideally suited to cruising either in small craft or in ships. The fjords cannot compare in length with Norway's, but they are just as complex, and lochs far in the heart of the mountains are tidal and ringed with seaweed. Granite contributes much less to the scenery of this region. Its heaviest concentration is the massif of Ben Nevis and its neighbours, which, like the Cairngorms, is not at first sight impressive although its 4,000 and more feet rear from the edge of the sea. Decidedly impressive, on the other hand, are the granite hills of the Isle of Arran, grouped about Goatfell, which lend a quality of fantasy to the Firth of Clyde. Most of the region's many peaks are of harder material: the metamorphic grits of Ben Ledi and Ben Lomond, the gabbro of the hills of Rum. But the major feature in determining the scenery is the series of long glens or straths opening south-westwards to

2 *Loch Broom, Ross and Cromarty*

the sea. Although a map of the coastline at once suggests that disintegration must be due to the enormous force of the Atlantic gales, this is not the case. The sea cannot make fjords. It is a century since Professor Geikie demonstrated that those fjords are old glens submerged beneath the sea, sunk in a fairly recent geological period, adding typically that "the tides now ebb and flow where of old there was the murmur of brooks and waterfalls". Some of the sea-lochs, as he pointed out, are actually deeper than the sea outside, Loch Fyne being a notable example. There appears to have been a sinking or tilting of the land-mass, when the sea moved in, and if one wants to gain a faint impression of this awesome spectacle it can be done by standing on the shore at Connel Ferry when the incoming tide rushes over the reef into Loch Etive with a roar like a river in spate. Those long glens, then, were the work of rivers like so many other valleys, and the deep-gouged basins like Loch Fyne and Loch Etive were shaped by subsidiary glaciers descending from the huge ice-field which lay upon Scotland in Pleistocene times. The hard rocks of the west, rising rapidly from sea or loch, have yielded little of the fertile ground gained from the sandstones in the east, and much of the soil in this region is a saturated peaty agglomeration of ancient mosses trapped in depressions in the rocks. It is too sour and wet to nourish even good heather, far less forests and crops, and the west as a whole is very wet, bearing the brunt of the humid winds of the Atlantic which bring a mild but drenching drizzle which at times seems to be unending. Yet climates are curiously local. They are determined by the hills, and one place may have an average rainfall comparable to the south of England's where another a few miles away records 100 inches. The low islands off the coast have the best of it, and it is well known that the sunshine on Tiree is so plentiful that crops ripen there as well as they do in the most fertile parts of England. The same contrasts apply with temperatures. On the top of Ben Nevis conditions are very nearly alpine, especially in corries which the sun never reaches; but on the other hand the warm waters of the North Atlantic Drift penetrate up the long arms of the sea-lochs and produce local climates so mild that winters may pass with little or no frost. Consequently, in this country of bare rock and bog one is constantly coming on some little paradise where the vegetation is exotic, and the shadow of palm, tree-fern or eucalyptus falls on the

3   *The Village of Glencoe, Argyllshire*

homely white-washed wall of cottage or farm-house. But grandeur, not homeliness, is the stuff of the beauty of the West Highlands, and what the visitor remembers is the menace of thunderclouds hanging on Buchaille Etive Mor, the splendour of Jura or Rum floating in a sea of molten fire.

The North-west Highlands show a much wider range of contrast between east and west than do the other two regions. No county, not even Inverness-shire, can provide antitheses quite comparable to Easter and Wester Ross. The gateway to the North-west is Inverness, and through it one enters immediately upon a belt of Old Red Sandstone which follows the east coast, more or less, right up to Caithness. It is rather tame, pleasant country at first, with green fields and woodlands, and the Beauly Firth and later, at Conon Bridge, the Cromarty Firth frequently in sight. Much of it is good farming land, notably on the big promontory of the Black Isle which divides the two firths. But any of the roads leading westwards carries one swiftly into grand though gaunt country where the rocky bone of the earth is very near its skin and often lies bare. In this region several of the main penetration routes are not towards the south-west but to the north-west: magnificent routes by way of Loch Shin, Strath Oykell or over the bleak moor of the Dirrie Mor, all of them leading to scenery which is as strange and arresting as it is fascinating to the geologist. When one descends to the coastal belt the crystalline rocks of the central area give place to the even more ancient Archaean rocks and the massive Torridonian formations which provide the landscape with extravagant variations, ranging from the savage red precipices of An Teallach, near Dundonell, to the eerie, lone peaks of Stac Polly and Quinag, Canisp and Suilven—especially, perhaps, Suilven, "The Pillar", that strangest of all Scottish hills which thrusts 2,000 feet of Torridon sandstone up from the tumbled moors around it. The eastern margin of this belt of country is defined by the Moine Thrust, in which along a line of about 100 miles the older schists in places have been forced over younger formations. In many places not even the passing of millions of years has won vegetation a lodging on the iron-hard gneisses and quartzites of this barren belt, and one thinks of the heathery Cairngorms as a garden by comparison. Yet so varied are the Highlands that even in this wilderness there are pockets of contrast in which the fields are green and flocks grow fat.

24

Anyone passing south on the road through Assynt will come upon them with astonishment. They are due to the occurrence of the Durness limestones, which have sweetened the sour land. In other parts of this corner of the Highlands generations of crofters have tried to achieve the same sweetening of the sour land by ferrying boatloads of shell-sand from the white beaches which fringe some of the islands, and the green patches on dark hillsides endure long after the cottages have crumbled and their tenants gone to some other part of the world. It is a hard country to live in. And it is less favoured, too, than the West Highlands are by mild sea currents, no doubt because the currents are diverted by the Isle of Skye past the mouths of Loch Torridon and Loch Broom and the other long sea-lochs which might otherwise have warmed a little the winter climate of the coast. The Lewisian gneiss which under-lies so much of the North-west is full of crevices and depressions which the heavy rainfall has filled with water and time has choked with sedge and peat to form the tarns and lochans which on the one-inch survey map show up like lace; and it is cold, dank, useless water with none of the vital sparkle of the streams that drain the hills. On the west side, this is a sub-arctic region. The east side, on the other hand, which includes the flattish lands of Caithness, has good grazing in plenty and can claim some of the largest sheep-flocks in the kingdom. On the coast the sandstones which underlie and yield these pastures disintegrate with dramatic effect, clawed out by storms which throw them back on land in a chaos of enormous blocks. On the north coasts of Caithness and Sutherland is some of the most spectacular cliff scenery to be found anywhere. These coasts front the narrow Pentland Firth where the Atlantic and the North Sea surge this way and that, and when gales pile up the waters against the land the effects would satisfy the most romantic sea-painter of the nineteenth century. The western coasts of Ross and Sutherland are in some degree shielded by the Hebrides from the full impact of the Atlantic storms, but on the north there is nothing between those precipices and the polar ice.

The people who live in those three regions are as different from one another as are the regions. The conventional idea of a Highlander is no more typical of the area which we are choosing to call the Highlands than Ben Nevis is typical of all the scenery.

Take, first, the Grampian region. Linguistically, most of this is not

Highland at all. If the trace of a Celtic accent seems to linger in the soft tones of Aberdeenshire, Banff and Moray, in fact Northern Scots is the speech of all three counties and its use extends well up the valleys of all the main rivers in this Grampian region: Tay, Dee, Don, Deveron, Spey and Findhorn. Northern Scots, it should be explained, is a variety of Lowland Scots, like English a dialect of Germanic origin, as distinct from the Gaelic speech which belongs to a completely different family. So in modern times not only the coastal plain of the north-east, but the glens of east Perthshire, of Deeside and Donside and of lower Strathspey speak a Lowland tongue. Even Tomintoul, highest village in the Highlands, speaks the Lowland dialect classified as Mid-Northern Scots! Speech, however, is somewhat misleading, for the Scots tongue has made a steady advance inland from the coast over a long period. This is partly due to the fact that nearly all the important towns in the region are on the coast, where Scots has been spoken since early times, but another reason which has been claimed is the readiness with which the Celt picks up foreign tongues, so that wherever there is a frontier between Celt and Saxon it is always the Celt and not the Saxon who becomes bilingual and the Celtic tongue, in this case the Gaelic, gradually retreats before its rival.

There was a time, of course, when the whole of the region was Celtic. The fertile low lands of all the coastal belt are sprinkled with wonderful carved stone monuments, mostly quite small, which archaeologists now agree to be the work of the Picts, the Painted Men, and the Picts were Celts, clearly with the Celtic gifts for imagery and decorative art. But the coast here as in East Anglia was exposed to raiders from the other side of the North Sea and it also drew immigrants from the south, so that the Celt, like his language, was either driven westward or dominated by the intruding Sassenach—which is to say Saxon—element. The coastal strip from the Tay right round to Inverness, and particularly the great rocky shoulder of it known as Buchan, has throughout historical times been inhabited by an industrious, tough, rugged people, not very easy to get to know, but staunch and warm-hearted. A high proportion of them even now are fisher folk, many of whom like the Close Brethren keep themselves very much to themselves, and great fleets have been based on Stonehaven and Arbroath, on Aberdeen of course, on Peterhead, on Fraserburgh and

Macduff, on Buckie, Lossiemouth and Burghead. All of them have suffered in competition with the highly-capitalised fleets from further south and from the foreigners who do not scruple to raid the inshore waters of the Moray Firth; but Aberdeen is still one of the country's great fish-markets and men from these fishing ports range far into Arctic and Atlantic waters. It is a coast which has to bear both easterly and northerly gales, and the people who live on it have grown hard-bitten and uncompromising. They tackle their farming in the same spirit, which they have need to do, for good land though the parishes of Kincardineshire and Buchan have they have also probably the bitterest winters of anywhere in Scotland. Snow can lie for a long time on the fields by the Ythan and the Deveron. But they build well in those parts, in every sense. It is not only because it is quarried so near that granite is still often used for ordinary houses, and it always seems to me there is less jerry-building in Aberdeenshire than elsewhere. The north-easterners' uncompromising attitude, coupled with a certain isolation, has made them resistant to innovations, and it was no freak of history that made Buchan a stronghold of episcopacy from the Reformation on. Among the fisher folk it is true there is revivalism, but on the whole it tends to be sombre, not emotional. The traditional imputation that Aberdeen is humourless is, however, quite unfounded. The Buchan dialect and its neighbour dialects are peculiarly suited to a pithy, salty kind of humour, although a good deal of what is said—the famous tale of the Turra' Coo is a case in point—loses nearly everything in translation.

In the upland portion of the Grampian region there is a sparse population, although much less sparse than in the remote west and north of Scotland. Its main concentrations are in Strathdee, Strathdon and Strathspey. The chief industry in those straths is catering for tourists, but it is evidence that one is in a countryside with Celtic roots that there is neither servility nor vulgarity in the conduct of tourism here, except when it is organised from the distant south. There is a tweedy character about the inhabitants, and in Ballater, for example, or Grantown-on-Spey, there is often in the conversation a breath of the great estates which surround them. On Deeside of course they do cultivate for retail purposes anecdotes about the Royal estates, but for the most part it is done with perfect taste and with complete respect and even affection. Their loyalty to the Queen and her family is loyalty to a laird rather than to a distant Sovereign, and a similar relationship with the landed estates survives at least partially all over this magnificent country of grouse moors and deer forests. It is not crofting country, except in so far as estate workers and foresters run their small-holdings as crofts. The land in the straths—and some of it is good land—is in the hands of small farmers where it is not part of the big estates.

The peoples of the West Highlands and the North-west can be considered as one. With the exception of Easter Ross and Caithness folk, they are of predominantly Gaelic stock. The change in type between those east and west of a line drawn from Inverness down through, say, Laggan and the Moor of Rannoch must be apparent even to the least skilled observer: apparent both in speech and in manner, for the Buchan and all the other north-eastern dialects which are so hard for a southerner to understand give way to a rather formal but musical English, while behaviour grows gentler, more courtly, in fact much more in keeping with the conventional picture of the Highland-man. Speech is "school English". Except in some remoter parts this does not mean the speaker was brought up with the Gaelic and learned his English at school, simply that we have left the region where a dialect of English is native. The great central watershed of the High-lands, once called Druim Albann, in ancient times was a formidable barrier, reinforced by dense forests, now denuded, and by immense bogs, now largely drained, and the Scots who settled to the west of it were utterly different in their ways from the Picts who eventually made their home to the east. The Scots were Gaels from Ireland who settled in Argyll. Strangely enough, the more remote parts of the Highlands in the earlier centuries of the Christian era were more in touch with vital happenings on the Continent than was the eastern coastal belt, because the migration route between Spain, Ireland and Scandinavia—more astir than either France or Germany after the fall of Rome—lay round the north of Scotland. Rich hoards of Viking remains have been found in Orkney, Caithness and Skye, and caches of eastern coins which must have come by way of the trade route through Russia; and these restless expeditions constantly touched the com-munities of west and north Scotland. The Norse influence is specially strong. Orkneys and Shetlands are, of course, pure Norse, and the same is largely true of Caithness, but Inner and Outer Hebrides have also injections of Norse blood.

Environment may have had as much influence as race in forming the character of the Highlander of those parts. Almost the only good agricultural ground is in the alluvial deposits built up by the rivers at the heads of the sea-lochs, and most of it is sour at that, while lack of sun prevents crops from ripening. So the Gael divided his time between hunting the plentiful game, fishing in the dangerous though richly-stocked seas and, naturally, fighting. Like other hunting and warring tribes—the Red Indians, the Zulus—those Highlanders were a dignified, proud race. Blood and kinship were matters of high concern. The clan system which developed among them was almost inevitable, built upon allegiance to a chief, and through him to the *Ard-Righ Albann*, the King himself; which explains the extraordinary loyalty towards Charles Edward Stewart even after his defeat at Culloden when a price was on his head, and he a man few of them had ever seen until he landed with his handful of followers in Moidart.

Like all Celtic peoples, Gaels take readily to music and poetry, although their idiom is so much their own that it has made no great impact on the musical or literary worlds. The *ceilidh*, an intimate concert with spontaneous contributions of song and story, can still be found, but it has suffered by penetration of the radio and other enter-tainments, and a great tradition is kept alive by nostalgic city dwellers and other exiles, the standards of performance maintained by An Comunn Gaidhealach, the Gaelic Society. Here again, environment has had its effect. Nearly all the finest Gaelic poetry, even when it springs from Jacobite sentiment, is carried by the poet's response to his natural surroundings. Duncan Ban MacIntyre's *Ode to Ben Dorain* is full of lyrical word-pictures. Jacobite themes were favourites long after the 'Forty-five, and the same sort of nostalgia appears later in such memories of exile as The "Canadian Boat Song". Romantic melancholy is close-knit with Gaelic thought. This passionate but rather ineffective attachment may be bred by a homeland which has little to reward its sons with except an almost supernatural beauty. Beauty here is not so much a bloom upon ripeness as a divine illusion, a pearly sea-haze lit by the setting sun, making glorious some reef of barren rocks mirrored in a treacherous sea. To suggest, however, that Gaels are all dreamers, without men of purpose or action among them, would be a complete misrepresentation. The crofter-fishermen of the Minch are as tough and determined men as could be found, and there are no better pioneers overseas than those who have gone out from the glens of Wester Ross.

The coastal strip which includes Caithness and the Black Isle belongs with the south shore of the Moray Firth rather than with the North-west Highlands. Its sandstone soils breed sheep in Caithness and good crops further south, aided by the moderate rainfall. Why its people should be so markedly un-Gaelic is not obvious. As many as 250 years ago the inhabitants of the Black Isle were Protestant, when all their Highland neighbours were Catholic, and they spoke English at a time when Gaelic was general nearly everywhere beyond the Highland Line. They have been Sassenachs as far back as records take us. It may be, as some writers have maintained, that the farmer-settlers of Neolithic times made their way to the Black Isle by the Great Glen.

The visual arts and the architecture of the Highlands will be introduced through chosen examples in the chapters to follow, but this is perhaps the place for an outline sketch.

Native contributions are almost entirely confined to the pre-medieval period. Much of that, too, is the work of foreigners or settlers from other lands. The richest hoards which have been dug up are associated with the Vikings and are distributed round the coasts of the Moray and Pentland Firths and of the Hebrides. Metal is the medium of the most outstanding finds—rich brooches and sword-hilts —but some interesting bone-carvings include the Lewis chess-men, now divided between the National Museum of Antiquities of Scotland and the British Museum. Orkney and Shetland have been fruitful hunting-grounds. A hoard of ornaments, silver ingots and coins found in a rabbit hole by a boy at Skaill in Orkney in 1858 was not surpassed until another boy exactly a century later came upon the St. Ninian's treasure in Shetland. The stream of Celtic art coming over from Ireland is much more widely distributed in Scotland than the work of the Northmen, and a good deal of it falls within the Highland area. Banff-shire and Aberdeenshire have produced some splendid material, notably bronze armlets which are monumental in their strength of design. But native art of early times divides itself broadly into two schools: the Pictish work, best seen in the coastal belt of the Cairn-

gorm region, and the Scoto-Irish work of Argyll and the Inner Hebrides.
The Picts are talented in many respects, but they excelled as carvers of
animals, and some of their sculptured stones depicting bulls or deer
with mounted hunters, possibly of some significance now forgotten,
stand comparison with the world's masterpieces in this *genre*. Irish art
in the west had a longer life, spanning nearly 1,000 years, but it shares
its achievements with Ireland herself, and a few of them such as the
Book of Kells, now treasured in Dublin, appear to have returned across
the Irish Sea.

As to architecture, primitive pagan forms in the north are interesting
rather than beautiful. None stirs the imagination more than the brochs,
native to Scotland and mostly within the Highland area. These strong
towers are nearly all sited in commanding spots in lonely places, and
the heaviest concentration is in the north-east. No doubt the broch-
people are also responsible for the wheel-houses, unfortified dwellings
well planned to resist the western gales. The establishment of Christianity naturally brought with it its own traditions, and a king of the
Picts is recorded as demanding that the missionary clergy build him a
church in the Roman manner; but resources were slender in the
Highland area, and there were never many churches which could
compare with the best in the Lowlands, far less abroad. What they lack
in architecture, however, they often make up for in setting, and there
is a special delight in coming on a modest abbey ruin in some spectacular glen or overlooking a silver beach glistening with the wash of
Atlantic rollers. In castles, the Highlands are moderately rich. Few are
large, but many are beautiful in their own right, without their romantic
setting. The richest countrysides boast the most elaborate examples,
and the vernacular style developed with conspicuous success in
Aberdeenshire and in Angus. To this heritage the Victorians, of course,
contributed their granite "copies", which have a certain unintended
charm of their own. Good domestic buildings in the vernacular
manner are not so common as further south, but there are some
excellent examples in Aberdeen, Elgin, Dunkeld, Dunblane, Inveraray,
as will be seen.

Passing mention has been made of how much more inaccessible the
Highlands were in ancient times. Dense forests, immense stretches of
swamp had to be faced in addition to barriers of mountain and sea-loch.

Greater forest areas imply heavier rainfall, with swollen streams and rivers and deeper swamps and, if writers of Roman times are reliable, mists and unhealthy exhalations perpetually hid the sun. Such conditions would encourage malarial mosquitoes—the "ague" which we hear of down to the nineteenth century must often have been malaria—and there were many wild animals since become extinct, such as the wolf, the bear, the wild boar and the formidable aurochs. The history of the Highlands is largely a history of their inaccessibility, a struggle between those who protected themselves and their way of life within this natural fortress and those who tried to reduce and tame them. The struggle lasted from remotest prehistoric days almost until the dawn of the twentieth century.

One must begin history somewhere, and in most British history books the starting point is the coming of the Romans. In A.D. 81 Agricola led an army to the Forth–Clyde line, where he set up a chain of forts; and then, provoked by Pictish threats or merely by curiosity, he probed further north by way of Perthshire and Strathmore until he brought the Pictish leader, Calgacus, to battle at Mons Graupius, which has given us the name of Grampian. The precise location of Mons Graupius is much in dispute, although it probably lay somewhere in the narrowed coastal strip near Stonehaven. It was a Roman victory. We know Agricola subsequently sent a fleet round the north of Scotland, but how far he and his successors carried his arms on land is a tantalising problem, for the evidence of Roman penetration becomes thinner and thinner, as we go up into Aberdeenshire and wheel left to the Moray Firth. Much later Severus again carried the eagles into the north. But we have reason to think the Picts developed by contact with Rome. Certainly they were strong enough as a nation to be the chief instrument of her overthrow in the north. What we should be careful to discount is the picture of a wilderness tenanted by painted savages; for Pictland—Strathmore, Angus, Aberdeenshire and Moray, at least—was a proud country bred not only in the arts of war but in the sophisticated tradition of Late Celtic culture, and at the same time its people were quite familiar with the ways of the great Imperial province to the south. There are indications that the Picts may have used Roman coinage, and it is not unlikely that their leading men spoke Latin at least as well as British statesmen do French. This people has

4 Loch Duich and the Five Sisters of Kintail, Ross and Cromarty

left no written records for our historians, but that does not mean they were inarticulate, for, as Dr. W. Douglas Simpson has said, the uniformity of their symbols and their widespread system of ideographic art is an astonishing manifestation of their genius.

At the collapse of the Roman empire, all the Highlands were Pictish. South Scotland was fairly well divided between the pagan Saxon invaders in the east and the Britons who had fled north from the collapsing Roman province. Rome had of course been Christian, and a new Christian Roman invasion of the Highlands took place about the beginning of the fifth century, with St. Ninian in place of Agricola. Many a carved stone is witness of his mission and of the missions of others who followed him, and these simple cross-carvings together with significant place-names mark the trail of christianisation as far as the Orkneys. The mission of St. Columba to Iona is more celebrated, but it did not take place until 563, a century and a half after Ninian's, and it seems in some part to have been a sort of counter-offensive against the Picts who had been driving the Scots, Columba's Irish kinsmen, from Argyll, then called Dalriada. Bangor, in Ulster, that rich training-ground of missionaries praised by St. Bernard, sent St. Moluag as far as eastern Pictland. The struggle between Scots and Picts went on until the ninth century, but the Picts were weakened by the increasing descents of the Northmen on their coasts, and at last in 844 Kenneth MacAlpine, a Scotic king with Pictish royal blood on his mother's side, became the first king of the two peoples, and in a sense the first King of Scotland. At the same time the spiritual centre of the kingdom was transferred from Iona to Dunkeld by the translation thence of Columba's relics to escape Norse depredations. This was a golden age in Highland history. Spiritually and politically, the north was Scotland, the Lowlands being a mere buffer against pagan Northumbria.

From the eighth to the twelfth century paganism battered at the frontiers of the Christian Highlands, mainly through unceasing Viking assaults round the coasts. The Hebrides, both Outer and Inner, the Shetlands and Orkneys and Caithness were all settled by those marauding worshippers of Odin. Meanwhile, the Celtic kingdom appears to have developed on lines of its own, and under Malcolm MacKenneth (1005–34) evolved a code of law, including a law of succession which is still the basis of Scottish practice. The vital part of "Scotland"

5–10 CROSSES AND CARVED STONES: (top row) *Iona; Sueno's Stone, Morayshire; Kilmory, Argyllshire.* (bottom row) *Kildalton, Islay; Glamis, Angus; Pennygown, Mull* continued to be the coastal belt of the Cairngorm region, but the last king to rule all Scotland from the north was Macbeth, an able ruler who, however, was frowned upon by the Church because he came to power by slaying Duncan. Macbeth in turn was slain and succeeded (1057) by Malcolm Canmore. He moved his capital south to Dunfermline, after which the Highlands more and more became the fringe of the kingdom and the Celtic element came under the political dominance of Saxon and Norman. Malcolm's queen, Margaret, conceived a special enmity for the Celtic Church. This in itself was a tragedy for the Highlands, for the Celtic Church was specially suited to the social system of north and west, its hereditary abbots closely bound up with the clans; but by about 1300 it survived only in the dwindling sect of Culdees, whose benefices the Roman Church systematically filled with her own priests.

From the close of the thirteenth century the strength of the Highlands lay in the developing clan system. Indeed, the spirit of fierce independence which stood Scotland in such good stead through the wars with England owed a great deal to this clan-family concept of feudalism. The King of Scots was still *Ard-Righ Albann*, the father of his great family, and when such a sovereign as David II made a progress in the north among his chieftains there was the happiest relationship, a relationship which David bequeathed to his nephew Robert II, first of that Stewart line which was to lean on Highland loyalty for nearly 400 years.

At first sight, politically and socially the Highlands of the Middle Ages seem as tattered and fragmentary as their outline on the map. Orkneys and Shetlands belong to the Northmen still, the Lords of the Isles hold sway in the Hebrides to a degree bordering on independence, the clans of the mainland are perpetually at feud. But the conventional picture of a strife-torn Highlands needing "civilising" is quite misleading, and Hume Brown long ago pointed out that Scotland had no internecine fighting on the scale of the Wars of the Roses in England or of the Burgundians and Armagnacs in France. The clan system of feudalism developed a certain basic stability which those other countries lacked, and its jealous regard for family tenures may well have produced a more advanced society, in which individual freedom found expression, than those societies threatened by predatory barons whom the King himself was often powerless to stop.

Yet the clan system provoked increasing suspicion and enmity. Before the Reformation the Church groped with a greedy hand for clan lands, while after 1560 the Reformed Kirk had nothing in common with the Highlanders, their colourful feudalism and their elusive Celtic approach to life being the antithesis of the soberly regulated system of the presbyteries. And the King himself, loyally as he was regarded by the Highlanders, found he had to curb their waywardness the more he came under the influence of English parliamentarianism. Royal burghs were established in the heart of the clan country, landholders were required to show their titles (1598), documents which few of them possessed, as the Government well knew. One company was actually formed in the Lowlands to colonise forfeited lands in "the barbarous Isle of Lewis", but had to retire, defeated; and indeed most attempts to weaken the clan system were defeated until the Union of the Crowns in 1603, when Lowlanders and English made common cause to bring enlightenment to the north. An Act of 1608 tried to dislocate the clan way of life by prohibiting certain weapons and boats. Further measures were imposed the following year, part religious, part economic, and a clause forbidding the sale of alcohol suggests measures to forbid the sale of "fire-water" to Red Indians! Whatever success the new laws had, the one material thing they failed to extract from their victims was their weapons, and for a long time the Highlander was to keep a sharp edge to his steel. Tribal feuds continued to be settled by blood down to 1688, when MacDonell of Keppoch revenged himself on the Mackintoshes over a land dispute. The Stewart kings were to find uses for the Highland Host's loyalty to the *Ard-Righ*. The clansmen were brought in, under Claverhouse, against the Covenanters, and then against William of Orange in 1688. Only after they formally received King James's sanction would they take the oath of allegiance to William, such were their old-fashioned feudal ideas of honour. The Government's notion of honour was different, as we know from the massacre in Glencoe of the MacDonalds by troops which had accepted their hospitality the night before. The Highlands were now quite disillusioned by the behaviour of a Crown which could have kept their loyalty. Again in 1715 the Stewarts appealed to their Highland followers and the standard was raised on the Braes of Mar. Mar was no leader. The cause failed, and failure was followed by repressive measures, among them the construction by General Wade of those strategic roads and bridges still to be seen in many places. The Stewart standard was raised for the last time in 1745 at Glenfinnan, when the appeal went out to "our faithful Highlanders, a people trained up and inured to arms". Charles Edward's progress through the glens was perfectly contrived to please the Celt's love of chivalry and pageantry. It is estimated that out of well over 20,000 clan warriors only about 8,000 sided with the Government, and it is no wonder that within a short time the Highland army put Scotland in the Prince's hands and saw him hold Court at Holyroodhouse. The same army could probably have won him the kingdom and installed his Court at St. James's; but in December the long retreat began which ended on 16th April at Culloden Muir.

The revenge taken by the Government on the Highlands is no doubt a measure of its terror for the Highlanders. Massacres beside which Glencoe pales took place in the glens. None claimed the price of £30,000 set on the head of the fugitive Charles Edward, although hundreds were in a position to betray the man they considered the son of their king. Disarming acts proscribed the possession of weapons, of Highland dress, even the bagpipes were classed as a weapon. The Crown claimed huge areas of the country. Exile was the fate of such rebels as escaped butchery or the gallows, but for the rest of the people began the long tale of emigration. Much of this was inevitable. Between the 'Forty-five and the end of the Napoleonic wars the population had almost doubled and was approaching the half-million—this in a land without means of agricultural expansion. The martial spirit was drawn off into newly-created Highland regiments of the British Army, a safety-valve device for which Lord President Forbes can claim the credit. The next chapter, however, is as discreditable to the Government as the massacres of 1746. Many of the chiefs were beguiled into moving south, becoming absentee landlords without means to maintain themselves in due style. Great tracts of the hills were turned into sheep-runs and rented to Lowland farmers backed by city financiers, whose rents went to the chiefs, and the miserable remnants of many a clan were driven off with extreme cruelty by the agents in these Clearances, the good land round the crofting townships being especially in demand. Dr. Johnson, that shrewd traveller and better friend of Scotland than he is often given credit for, remarked with regret on the resulting break-up, and particularly deplored the educating of chieftains in the south of England where, he said, "they will be tamed into insignificance".

The Highlands ceased to be a force in the affairs of the United Kingdom when the clans were disarmed, but it was the century of exploitation which followed that turned them into something like a wilderness. The exodus of families driven out by sheep became a torrent which greatly profited shipping agents, who did their best to keep it going. Again, the dislocated economy of the clan system became linked to fickle outside markets. Kelp, for example, provided a living for many on the coasts in the second half of the eighteenth century, but the market collapsed early in the nineteenth. Then deer forests ousted many of the sheep-runs, with a further wave of evictions. "Improvers", however, probably did as much damage as anyone, and such disciples of progress as the Duke of Sutherland, an early example of that type of planner who plans without first making a profound study of the society he proposes to re-model, brought misery to great areas. A succession of famines made things worse, many a chief who clung to the old clan-family tradition well-nigh ruining himself in the attempt to keep his clanspeople alive.

Upon this desolate scene dawned the Victorian age. It was to perpetuate the economy of the deer forest and establish the tradition of the grouse moor, and to scatter mock-baronial buildings in glen and strath; but it brought back at least an imitation of the clan-family pattern of living, and restored some of his dignity to the Highlander. The old Queen's memory is kept extraordinarily fresh on Deeside even to-day, much more than half a century after her passing. Whatever the reason for her first affection for the Highlands, the Highlanders responded at once to the feudal matriarchy which she established at Balmoral. Her passion for such trappings as tartan and her revival of the gatherings woke sympathy in the Celt, even if much of it seemed spurious to purists and objective observers, and she in turn was sympathetic to the needs of her people in the north. In her lengthier and lengthier residences at Balmoral she came to know hundreds of them and interested herself in their affairs, helped them, worshipped with them—more earnestly than His Grace of Canterbury of that time approved!—and came nearer than any sovereign had done for centuries to becoming a true *Ard-Righ Albann*, Chief among the chiefs. The things she did were simple and personal, in no way remedying political and economic wrongs, but they went straight to the heart of the Highland problem, and if Governments had been capable of such sympathy and intuitive understanding the problem might long ago have been resolved.

CHAPTER TWO

Dunblane and the Highland Border

We began this journey into the Highlands with a reconnaissance from the battlements of Stirling Castle. In spite of the peaks that ring its northern horizon, Stirling is in no sense a Highland town; so we shall come down from the battlements and cross the Forth and follow the road that no doubt Agricola followed, and a great many others after him who for one reason or another were drawn towards the northern hills. It is the natural approach to the Highlands. Like a sign-post, the monument to the memory of Sir William Wallace points the way on its crag, an outlier of the Ochil Hills. It is easy to mock at this "Gothick" tower, exhibiting as it does as Wallace's weapon a sword which is of a kind that did not come into being for many a generation after Wallace died; but the Wallace monument belongs with that romantic Balmoralism which has made its own sort of contribution to Highland tradition and is in any case now quite legally an antique in its own right.

The road winds round the base of the Ochils into Bridge-of-Allan, thence into Strathallan, where Dunblane lies among its trees and gardens, as snug a little cathedral town as can be found in the north. There is nothing Highland about it, but it lies at a junction of ways that lead straight into the hills, and there is no better or more pleasant centre for exploring the extreme southern foothills of the Highland massif.

At first sight it may seem strange that an important church should have been set right on the edge of a wild country inhabited by lawless tribes, but the same thing will be found again and again along the

41

Highland boundary, which is sprinkled with ancient holy places. Nearly always there is at least a carved stone or two, long antedating the church, like the old Celtic cross found under the nave at Dunblane, preserved at the west end of the north aisle. These stones are reminders that intractable as they were to the Romans and to the early kings of Scotland itself, the people who used the Highland hills as their refuge and stronghold were conquered easily and early by the Cross, although the cross was of their own shaping and was not quite the orthodox cross of Rome. It should not be forgotten, at the outset, that here in the far north in the Dark Ages Christianity was in an outpost cut off by pagan hordes from its source, and that it was out of northern fastnesses of which the Highlands were a flank that missionaries ventured south into Europe carrying their faith as far as Switzerland. I stress this because our historians have, perhaps naturally, paid more attention to assiduous foreign scribes such as Tacitus than they have to dumb stones weathering in kirkyards, unable to do more than hint at a culture and an ordered society. The Celtic Church survived in the sects of Culdees which persisted along the Highland border. Those holy men were tough. Their college at Dunblane, founded by St. Blane in the sixth century, survived fire and plunder by Briton and Dane.

From several points of view, the Cathedral Church of St. Blane is one of the most interesting in Scotland. It was David I, that "sair sanct for the crown", who erected Dunblane into a bishopric about 1150, and the first cathedral came into being during the half-century that followed, but the only part of this which has survived is in the lower portion of the tower. There was not enough money for its upkeep, and Friar Clement had to make a journey to Rome to secure the means to restore the roof. The cathedral suffered further heavy damage during the centuries that followed. Edward I ripped the lead from the roof for the siege-engines which he built to reduce Stirling Castle. It was desecrated by the Earl of Argyll in 1559, though he forebore to wreck the choir. As it stands now, the lower two-thirds of the tower is Norman, topped by a sixteenth-century addition, the nave is in the first Pointed style, the choir is a little later, and the north aisle or lady chapel comes in date somewhere between the tower and the nave. In spite of Argyll's depredations, the cathedral retains some very beautiful ornament. The west door, though simple, is richly and deeply moulded, and the three windows above it were singled out by Ruskin in a lecture to the Philosophical Institution of Edinburgh in words reminiscent of a passage in *The Stones of Venice*. Why, he asks, is that west window beautiful?—"Because in its great contours it has the form of a forest leaf, and because in its decoration he has used nothing but forest leaves. He was no common man who designed that cathedral of Dunblane. I know nothing so perfect in its simplicity, and so beautiful so far as it reaches, in all the Gothic with which I am acquainted . . . Instead of

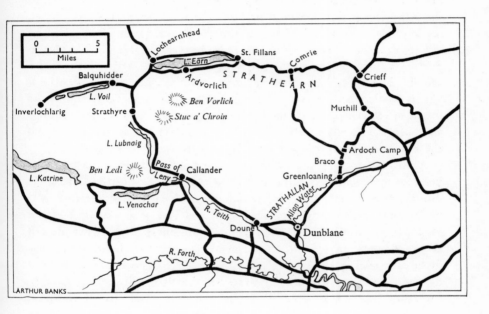

putting a mere formal dog's-tooth, as everybody else did at the time, he went down to the woody bank of the sweet river beneath the rocks on which he was building, and he took up a few of the fallen leaves that lay by and he set them in his arch side by side for ever."

The cathedral has another possession, unique in Scotland. It is a series of richly-carved, canopied choir stalls of the fifteenth century. They are known as the Ochiltree stalls, as nearby is an effigy of Bishop Ochiltree, who died in 1447. Only in King's College Chapel, in Aberdeen, is there anything comparable. Also fairly uncommon features in a Scots church are the recumbent stone effigies of Malise, eighth Earl of Strathearn, and his wife. In the floor of the north choir are three blue stones believed once to have covered the graves of Lady Margaret Drummond and her sisters. The story goes that James IV when a youth fell in love with Lady Margaret and secretly married her, and indeed had a daughter by her. When he came to the throne James prepared to make public his marriage, but a Court party had determined he should marry an English princess and, at the official wedding breakfast, Margaret and her sisters were poisoned. Broken-hearted, the King arranged a magnificent burial in the cathedral of which the uncle of the sisters, Sir Walter Drummond, was Dean.

Dunblane lies at the fork of two roads into the Highlands. One is the Perth road, following the Allan Water along the north fringe of the Ochils. The other makes for Callander and the blue peak of Ben Ledi which marks the pass into the MacGregor country. Both routes, as might be expected, are steeped in history, as most of the major comings and goings between south and north in the days before the estuary of the Forth had been bridged were by way of one or the other.

A few miles along the Callander road is the village of Doune. It is heralded by a small roadside sign on which a pair of crossed pistols is displayed, a cryptic sign which unfortunately only the initiated will understand. For a long time Doune played a very special part in the Highland economy, for it made some of the finest of the weapons and accoutrements in which the clansman's heart delighted. It was especially celebrated for its pistols, and this over a period of something like two centuries. The weapons made in this little village were latterly sometimes such masterpieces of the gunsmith's art that they found their way as presents to the most fastidious courts in Europe. They are preserved in the great museums abroad alongside the work of Lazzarino Cominazzo of Brescia himself: in the Musée d'Artillerie in Paris, in the Metropolitan Museum of Art in New York.

If I linger upon this little village and its products, it is not because any of the pistols can now be seen there—the roadside sign apart!—but because it reflects a significant aspect of Highland history: Celtic pride and love of putting on a brave show. Doune must in a way have been like some of those frontier towns in the western states of America to which Indian braves would come in search of pretty weapons which on occasion would be put to use against the frontiersmen themselves. The names of the great Doune pistol-smiths, Campbell and Caddell, Murdoch and Christie, are not all of them Highland, although their lives were devoted to supplying the Highlanders. The chief characteristic of the Doune pistol is that it is all-metal, butt, stock and barrel; but its lines are as delicately flowing as if it were carved in soft wood, and its engraved decoration is sometimes nearly as intricate as lace. Typically, the butt ends in a scroll or "ram's horn". There is no trigger-guard. Trigger and the pricker lodged between the horns of the butt have silver finials, and in the best specimens silver inlay is beaten into the surface decoration. In the rarest pieces of all gold takes the place of silver, but the only two such pairs I have seen or heard of are the Campbell pistols in the Royal collection at Windsor and a similar brace stolen some years ago from the Colville collection in Edinburgh Castle, now almost certainly in the United States. The pistols were usually made in pairs, with right- and left-hand locks. It may seem surprising that the basic metal from which the pistols were made was old horseshoe-nails, which were twisted into a crude chain and then hammered into a thick ribbon that was finally coiled and beaten round a metal rod of approximately the right bore.

The Disarming Acts which followed Prince Charles Edward's rebellion of the 'Forty-five did not immediately bring to an end the Doune pistol industry. This is surprising, as the proscriptions forbade any clansman to carry weapons, or even to wear the kilt or to play the bagpipes which, perhaps shrewdly enough, were, as we have seen, counted as a weapon of war. Doune must have got customers in the Lowlands, as there were smiths working there until the end of the eighteenth century, but the first *Statistical Account of Scotland*, compiled just before 1800, laments that when John Murdoch retires from business this traditional industry will be dead. In the end it received the compliment of having two classes of imitator. On the one hand there were the makers of those magnificent gilded and enamelled costume pistols of "Highland" appearance such as the Clanranald pistols in the National Museum of Antiquities or that inserted by Sir Henry Raeburn into his portrait of Macdonell of Glengarry in the National Gallery of Scotland. On the other is the numerous group of crude imitations supplied in quantity to the Highland regiments in the early days, frankly given away by the name on the lockplate—one Bissell, a Birmingham gunsmith! For those interested in a weapon which a French connoisseur has called "*un petit chef-d'œuvre de précision et de bon goût*", the most complete collection of Doune pistols is to be found in the National Museum of Antiquities in Edinburgh, but there are extensive collections also in the Royal Scottish Museum and in the Kelvingrove Museum in Glasgow, and there are several also in the armouries of the Tower of London.

Doune is a pleasant village at the junction of the Ardoch burn with the River Teith, but its chief attraction now is the castle. There are many castles in and about the Highlands, but to make a point of inspecting even those within sight of the main routes would be a lengthy and not necessarily always a rewarding business. Doune Castle, however, must be impressive even to someone with no knowledge of the finer points of medieval fortifications. It stands right above the junction of the two waters. It has tremendous frontal strength, and must have needed no pennons flying from the battlements to proclaim it to the stranger as the stronghold of some personage of great power. The man who built it was in fact the Regent of Scotland, Murdoch, second Duke of Albany, who held the country during the English captivity of James I, and the time of its building was the end of the fourteenth century. It combines great military strength with the extensive accommodation demanded by an owner of royal rank, and those two requirements are married in the extraordinary north-east tower, which even in its present state is 80 feet in height. The low, narrow entrance at the base of the tower is, of course, a concession to strength; but inside and above the entrance is a baronial hall 35 feet long with a great double fireplace, a chamber which, hung with arras and suitably furnished, must have had considerable grandeur. And it was to accommodate more than one great figure in history in the centuries after Duke Murdoch paid for treachery with his head on the castle-hill of Stirling. In 1502 Doune was given in life-rent to Margaret Tudor, daughter of Henry VII of England and wife of James IV of Scotland. It was a favourite residence of Mary Queen of Scots. In the 'Forty-five it had a Jacobite garrison, and committed to it were several prisoners from the field of Falkirk, among them the Rev. John Home, the minister who scandalised the Kirk by writing for the theatre.

Enterprising even in captivity, Home escaped down the formidable battlements of Doune Castle by knotting together the bed-clothes.

As one goes westwards out of Doune towards Callander, Ben Ledi, the Hill of God, rears like a gatepost of the narrow pass leading to the western Highlands. Beyond the Pass of Leny, to the left of the road, the shoulder of the Ben plunges into the long, narrow waters of Loch Lubnaig. Here begins that quite small tract of the Highlands over which Sir Walter Scott dropped a golden veil. Scott was a Lowlander of Lowlanders. He built a stage for romances on this threshold of the Highlands and put on drama after drama against the back-drop of poignantly beautiful lochs mirroring mountain-sides on which the hanging birchwoods are breath-catching in their colours, whether the tender greens of spring or the flame of autumn. It all seems rather obvious to us to-day, even the picture-postcard beauty of these lochs and hills which connoisseurs pass by on their way to remoter, less homely types of Highland scenery; and the dramas of Scott, with their stags and their ragged caterans and Robin-Hood figures, are a little out of fashion in an age which knows well that the Highlands are a depressed area and have been so for centuries. Every time one comes here, therefore, it is to suffer a pleasurable shock at the rediscovery of how splendid this all-too-accessible country is.

The man who stands out as the embodiment of the old clansman, with all his good and his bad points, is of course the Rob Roy immortalised by Scott. A few miles beyond Loch Lubnaig, in a lovely glen, a side-road strikes off westwards to Loch Voil, and in the churchyard of Balquhidder village is the grave of Rob Roy. It is a modest grave for one who created such a stir, but the very fact that Rob was able to die peacefully in his bed in the heart of his home country itself typifies his blend of cunning with courage.

> *The eagle, he was lord above,*
> *And Rob was lord below.*

The eagle still lords it above the Braes of Balquhidder, for there is a long-established eyrie in at least one of the wild glens on the loch-side, and the legend of Rob continues to lord it over the whole of this MacGregor country as Robin Hood's does in Sherwood forest. In making Rob into a bit of a Robin Hood, Scott was not romanticising

47

entirely, but there was a great deal of the rascal in the man, and he inherited a long tale of ancestral trouble-making which brought letters of fire and sword to be issued against "the wicked clan Gregor, so long continuing in blood, slaughter, theft and robbery", as a document of 1558 has it. Rob was of the stuff of heroes of fiction. On the one hand, he was decently educated and had a proper respect for learning; on the other, he had a splendid physique and was a masterly swordsman with a phenomenal reach which made him truly formidable in a fight. He possessed the lands of Inversnaid and Craig Royston, and set out to be respectable enough as a cattle dealer and stockman; but unhappily reavers from the north raided his herds and forced him to recruit a band of protective guards, and after a time he began to lend those protectors, for a consideration, to his neighbours. Soon he was extorting dues from all and sundry, an elaborate system of blackmail which landowners in the district tried to evade at their peril. Not that his neighbours showed him any particular scruples when chances arose, and a web of feuds and acts of vengeance was spun which had him entangled throughout most of his life. He took sides in the quarrels of the great families of the west, notably the Montroses and the Argylls; but the event which got him into greatest danger was the rebellion of 1715, in which he sided with the Jacobites and was an officer in the Pretender's army at the battle of Sheriffmuir. Here the wily Rob remained on a hill with his clansmen and watched the battle, not out of cowardice, but because of the friendly sentiments which he had for the general on the other side, Argyll. Edinchip, the house of the MacGregor of MacGregor to-day, which is only a few miles along the road from Balquhidder, possesses a seventeenth-century powder-horn with the inscription LORD · THOV · ME · DEFEND · FROM · SUBTIL · SORT · OF · THOSE · THAT · FRIENDSHIP · ME PRETEND · AND ARE · MY · MORTAL · FOES. I have sometimes wondered if Rob ever contemplated this horn. But this cunning of his stood him in good stead when the Government set a price of £1,000 on his head, for somehow he escaped both scaffold and exile. The spiritual course which he steered was subtle too. Born a Presbyterian, as a friendly gesture towards the Earl of Perth, he turned to Rome, yet so lightly did he regard his adopted faith that, as Scott records, he commented that extreme unction was "a great waste of oil".

Just north of the policies of Edinchip is the village of Lochearnhead. Here one may circle back again towards Dunblane by turning east along the shore of Loch Earn, and one can avoid the hustle of buses and tourist cars which plague this country in the season by choosing the minor road that hugs the south shore, skirting the base of Ben Vorlich which, with its close neighbour, Stuc a Chroin, is the first "Munro" along this road into the Highlands. A Munro is a summit of 3,000 feet or more. The name commemorates the first man to climb all such summits in Scotland, a considerable achievement, as there are 543 of them. Close by the road here is Ardvorlich House. This is the seat of the Stewarts of Ardvorlich, which Scott in *The Legend of Montrose* described as "Darnlinvarach Castle". It is steeped in history, the most violent chapter of which is given at length in *The Legend*; but I will linger on it here for a moment because it is the home of the most celebrated of all Highland charm-stones, that odd group of relics which I have described at length in another book. These stones are rock-crystals of magical repute, used for curing everything from cattle-sickness to the whooping-cough, but sometimes associated with witchcraft. The stone at Ardvorlich, known as the Clach-Dearg or the Red Stone, is secured with hoops of silver and fitted with a chain. The tale is that it came from the East with the Crusaders, but, like others of its kind, it seems to be one of the beautiful quartz crystals which may be come by among the Highland hills. The *Statistical Account* romantically ascribes it to the Druids, but more interestingly records that even in its time people all over the district were resorting to it as "a sovereign remedy in all diseases of cattle".

St. Fillans, the village at the east end of the loch, commemorates a man who evangelised all the country hereabout. He was greatly venerated in the Middle Ages: locally, for many associations, among them a healing spring near the village, a spring which in protest at the Reformation removed itself for some obscure reason from the top of a hill to its foot; and nationally, for the aid which he gave his country when it lay under the threat of subjugation. St. Fillan was the favourite saint of Robert the Bruce, who believed his life had been saved by him at the battle of Dalrigh. On the field of Bannockburn the saint was again invoked in the shape of his arm-bone. There is, however, a surviving relic associated with him, the beautiful Quigrich or crozier bearing his

49

name, now in the National Museum of Antiquities. In a letter of James III dated 6th July, 1487, the custodians of the Quigrich are named as one Malise Doire and his progenitors, of Strathfillan. Doire is an early spelling of Dewar, and the English traveller, Pennant, saw the Quigrich in the possession of a labourer called Dewar in 1782. Subsequently a member of the family emigrated to Canada and took the object with him, until in 1876 the National Museum procured it. It consists of an outer case of gilt silver, finely wrought, and probably fifteenth-century work, containing the bronze crozier-head proper, which is much earlier in date.

At this point, with Strathearn stretching away eastwards toward the distant Tay, and with the peaks of Breadalbane to the north-west, we are about midway along the great Highland Border Fault. The broad strath with its fertile fields and pastures and woodlands is part of the belt of Lower Old Red Sandstone which crosses all Scotland diagonally, and the peaks that serrate the north-western horizon, forming the barrier that determined the course of Scottish history from the days of Agricola onwards are massed formations of hard quartzites and schists with some knobs of diorite and granite. At this midway point is the village of Comrie. Comrie is of course famed as Scotland's earthquake centre. The village wears its reputation lightly: indeed, the reputation may even contribute to its popularity as a holiday resort, for there have been no very terrifying manifestations for a long time. The quakes are a reminder that Lowlands and Highlands belong to quite different geological ages, and that even the passage of many millions of years has not quite bonded the two. Their occurrences are rare, but some relatively severe shocks are on record. Perhaps the worst was in 1839, when the entire district shuddered and a tremendous subterranean roar was heard, "like a hundred pieces of ordnance discharged at once", and people in Comrie fainted and ran into the streets and churches were opened for prayer.

Mention of Agricola is a reminder that the road from Dunblane up into this broad strath of the Earn is the road the Romans took in the furthest probe north they ever made on land. There is a chain of Roman camps and stations and the traces of roads from Strathallan out across Strathearn. It may be an odd fancy, but I find those innocent-looking mounds and grassy ditches in sight of the Highland hills more

impressive evidence of the might of Imperial Rome than the monuments in the heart of Rome itself.

With the Ochils on one side and the outliers of the Highland hills on
the other, Strathallan is the narrow place through which in former
days all traffic must pass between the south and the open country along
the north-east coast, so it is scarcely surprising to find here the finest
example of a Roman camp in all Scotland. From Dunblane, one turns
off the Perth road into the Crieff road at Greenloaning. Braco is the
modern village nearest the camp, which is in the grounds of Ardoch
House. Sir George Macdonald, who was the Grand Old Man among
students of Roman Scotland, said that Ardoch "remains in its decay
more impressive than any other Roman fort in Scotland". It presents
an extraordinary complex of ridges and ditches, partly due to the fact
that there were Roman structures here at two different times. Some
wonderful detective work has been done among the ridges and ditches.
There was a period when the buildings of the camp were of wood,
probably in Agricola's time, although the only evidence is some post-
holes and deposits of charcoal. Later, in Antonine's day, there were
stone buildings. It is thought the Romans gave the name Alauns to the
fort, a name mentioned by Ptolemy and perhaps derived from the rocky
river Allan close by. In later times there have been many legends about
the camp, including the inevitable tale of buried treasure:

> *From the camp of Ardoch*
> *To the Grinnin hill of Keir*
> *Are nine Kings' rents*
> *For seven hundred year.*

This ancient rhyme once induced a local court to offer his life to a
criminal they had condemned if he would descend a deep hole by the
praetorium of the camp. He agreed and was let down on a rope. When
he was drawn up he brought with him a collection of Roman helmets
and weapons, so the story goes, but on his second descent after the
elusive treasure he died from the foul air. There does appear to have
been such a hole until about 1720, but a local sportsman is believed to
have filled it in to prevent hares escaping from his dogs.

There was a time when the celebrated battle of Mons Graupius was
said to have been fought around here, the critical battle at which

Tacitus recorded the defeat of Calgacus and his Caledonians. In the latest view Mons Graupius, so commonly made the origin of the name Grampian, is placed right away at the other end of Strathmore. Wherever it may have been, Agricola and his legions, with his son-in-law busily recording events on his tablets, once tramped these straths and scanned for signs of lurking Caledonian outposts the blue barrier of the Grampians which they never attempted to penetrate.

CHAPTER THREE

Perth and the Central Highlands

Perth is one of the best strategic centres in Scotland. The Romans recognised this, from the military standpoint; the Picts, and later the Scots themselves, saw it as a natural political capital; and the visitor bent upon being within easy reach of as many interesting and pleasant places as possible must soon discover he can make no better choice than Perth.

I will spare the reader the usual reference to the Roman comparison between Tay and Tiber. Indeed I would doubt that the Tungrians and Batavians and others who made up the legions in these parts had ever set eyes on the Tiber. But whatever words the sight drew from them, the first glimpse of Tay from the high ground south of Perth must have given the weary legionaries a moment of pleasure. The setting is splendid—a far rim of blue hills ringing a vast pleasance of green fields and woods, with the bends of the river flashing silver in the sun. Even in the days of the Roman, smoke would be rising from the fires of a settlement, as it rises from hundreds of chimney pots to-day, for half a dozen major routes converge on this spot, and the river itself is wide and slow and almost within scent of the sea and its highways.

Perth has only 40,000 inhabitants, but it is one of the five cities of Scotland whose civic heads are entitled to be called Lord Provost. In precedence it ranks before all other burghs in the country, except Edinburgh. This is a pointer to ancient dignity. Perth was capital of Scotland long before Edinburgh, and although there is little left to remind us of such a time there is a spaciousness here and an air of quality in many of the buildings quite foreign to towns which owe their being to industrial expansion or commerce alone.

The old name for Perth was St. John's Town, modified to St. Johnstone, and the core of it, its oldest building, is the kirk of St. John the Baptist, the crown steeple of which can be seen above the roofs for several miles. Not that even this church can be called medieval, for a good part of it was rebuilt in the eighteenth century. Nave and transept, however, are substantially thirteenth, and the choir is fifteenth, as the steeple is. The church has kept enough of its character to make it easy to remember that here on 11th May, 1539, Knox thundered forth those denunciations of clerical corruption which loosed the passions of the "rascal multitude". Here in St. John's the first blow in the battle of the Reformation in Scotland was struck: not, technically, by a Reformer, but by a priest incensed at a boy who called him an idolator. The boy's reply, a stone, was aimed at the priest but missed him and hit the "glorious tabernacle" on the high altar. This began the rioting, and the mob seized upon "the monuments of idolatry".

It is a strange thing that in St. John's, where the Reformers' destruction of church panoply began, survives the only collection of pre-Reformation plate in any Scottish church. Exhibited in a glass case in the church are the "Queen Mary" and the "Nuremberg" cups—fine standing cups of silver-gilt, German pieces of Mary Queen of Scots' time—and with them two handsome London steeple-cups of the reign of Mary's son, James VI and I. Tradition has it that the "Mary" cup was found in the street after the rioting in the church and concealed by a woman in her father's grave, but Mary herself is unlikely to have been the donor as she never visited Perth until after the Reformation broke in 1560. That the donor might have been her mother, Mary of Guise, is at least possible. And with those rich pieces in the case is a superb parcel-gilt silver baptismal basin made by David Gilbert of Edinburgh near the close of the sixteenth century, one of the loveliest things which have come down to us from the earlier Scottish goldsmiths, with the pure lines characteristic of the oldest church plate of the Reformed fashion.

The Perth of Knox's day and before survives mainly in a few ancient place-names, such as Castle Gable. If the old buildings have gone, however, early nineteenth-century Perth provides a good picture of a

Scottish country town of the period, with many mellow neo-classical buildings nicely disposed. Tay Street, facing the river and with a tree-shaded pavement, possesses some handsome public buildings, but the best houses are in the terraces overlooking the North Inch, one of the two historic parks which are the town's principal features. Unhappily the houses are of soft stone and many of their details have weathered away. Functionally they are out of date; but the façades at least are worth preserving, for without them the Inch, in spite of its bright green sward and its white-flannelled cricketers in season, would be undefined.

Cricket seems a little out of place in the heart of Pictland, but in fact cricket on the Inches is almost as much a part of the scene as the background of classic grey buildings. Cricket took root in this Highland soil in an odd way as much as a century and a half ago, and it has been said the man responsible for its coming was Napoleon. A great number of French prisoners were sent to Perth—the present convict prison beside the South Inch was built in 1812 to house them—and with them came their guards, who included a Hussar regiment from England. Inevitably the Hussars turned the Inch into a cricket-ground and in no time they had converted the local men to the game. Perth, therefore, appears to be the birthplace of cricket in Scotland. Fittingly, the Perth club has an honourable record, counting among its victims not only an All-Scotland eleven but also I Zingari. Yet the two Inches have been settings for sporting events far back into history. In the later Middle Ages the usual royal decrees promulgated that frivolous pastimes such as golf and football be "utterly cried down" to promote more archery practice; but by 1502 it was otherwise, for the exchequer accounts of James IV contain an item in that year: "To the bowar of Sanct John-stoune, for golf clubs, xiiiis." The sixth James also played on the Inches, and has given his name to a golf club which still exists.

In 1396 the North Inch resounded to strokes noisier than bat on ball. There was bitter dispute between two groups of Highlanders said to have belonged to the clans Chattan and Kay. It was agreed to decide the issue by means of a fight between 30 men chosen from each side. A tremendous gallery, which included Robert III and his queen as well as English and foreign nobles, assembled to watch the outcome. Clan Chattan lacked one man and, as Sir Walter tells in *The Fair Maid of*

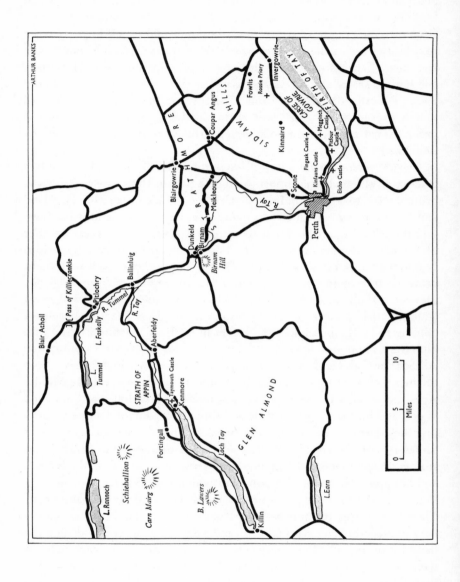

Perth, the town's armourer, Hal o' the Wynd, offered his services. The battle was a dreadful one and the turf was drenched in blood, but eventually only a single man of Clan Kay survived, and the 11 Chattan men left were too sorely hurt to follow when he threw himself into the Tay and swam to safety. Although sometimes represented as an illustration of the rather disreputable ways of Highland caterans, the battle of the North Inch is now more often accepted as a case of a decision legitimately arrived at under the code of feudal chivalry. The clansmen were merely doing something which was accepted practice in the pages of Froissart's *Chronicles*. In the Highlands this way of thinking had not really died in the eighteenth century. Indeed, the behaviour of Alistair Macdonell of Glengarry, described in Chapter Eight, suggests it was not entirely dead even in the nineteenth.

It is distressing that a town with such a stirring history of kings and parliaments should have nothing left to show for it. Parliament Close commemorates the house in which so many Scottish parliaments were held until the fifteenth century, a house removed only 150 years ago. Royal visits were many down to the year 1437, when the poet-king, James I, was slain in the Monastery of the Black Friars by Sir Robert Graham and a great band of assassins from the north. The tale of Catherine Douglas barring the door with her arm and of the final struggle in the cellar is well known, but the monastery is gone. It used to stand behind the Fair Maid's House.

It is not Perth itself which held such importance for Scottish kings, but Scone, two miles away on the road to Blairgowrie. All Scots schoolchildren know, or should do, that the kings of Scotland were crowned at Scone, although not one in a thousand could venture a good guess as to the significance of this. The Scone ceremony had its origin 12 centuries ago, when Scone was the capital of the Pictish kingdom. The Picts were conquered by the Cross more completely than they were ever conquered by the sword; but it was not the plain cross of Rome which they set up among them but their own strange version associated with a symbolism never satisfactorily explained, as we shall see in another place. The lost rituals of the Scone coronations had their roots deep in the Pictish past, and drew some sort of ancient strength from this. Probably Edward I understood such things better than we do. His sacking of the abbey at Scone was no common pillaging, but a search for the token of his enemy's resistance. The most precious possession of the abbey was the Stone of Destiny, supposed to be the receptacle of Scottish strength. Legend had it the Stone was the pillow on which Jacob rested his head when he had his vision, and which was said to have come by way of Spain to Ireland, thence to Dunstaffnage in Argyll, from which it was brought to Scone by Kenneth MacAlpine, uniter of Scotland, about the year 843. Kenneth chose Scone because it was here the Picts had their chief centre, and here he defeated them.

The Stone itself, which Edward carried off in 1297 and placed in Westminster Abbey—thereby, according to believers in its legendary power, depositing a Trojan horse in the midst of the Sassenachs—is a piece of the Old Red Sandstone common enough in Scotland and quarried in quantity in the neighbourhood of Scone itself. This may mean anything or nothing. Doubts have been cast on Edward's prize at various times, and after the notorious abduction of the Stone from Westminster a few years ago an amusing, learned and persuasive argument against its being the real thing was published by a distinguished archaeologist and former Inspector of Ancient Monuments, Dr. James Richardson. He compared the quarry-dressed block at Westminster with early medieval accounts of Scottish coronations and with representations on royal seals, and could find no point of correspondence between the plain stone and the royal seats on which the kings were crowned. In view of Pictish skill at stone carving, it is certainly odd that a relic of such significance should go unadorned, and Henningburgh's account of the stone on which Balliol was crowned at Scone only a few years before Edward's invasion says it was "hollowed out and fashioned in the manner of a round chair". Whatever the truth, Dr. Richardson concluded his essay by suggesting the true Stone was hidden away by the Abbot of Scone at the approach of the English king, and he remarks it as odd that the Scots showed no enthusiasm when, on two occasions, the English offered to return the Stone.

Much as romantic painters and writers like to site their castles on lonely, inaccessible crags, real castles are much more often set among the fat lands that can provide a comfortable existence; and as these strongholds gathered great events about them, history is made among the hedges and haystacks more often than among savage mountains. It

58

11   Schiehallion across Loch Rannoch, Perthshire

is easy to illustrate this up and down the Highlands and their border-lands. Nowhere can it be done more neatly in the space of an afternoon than by following the Tay out of Perth on the Dundee road. Swinging round Kinnoull Hill, one comes to a narrow stretch of rich fields and woods hemmed in between the river and the spurs of the Sidlaw Hills. This neck of land leads out into the celebrated Carse of Gowrie. The land is a rich, open soil made up of alluvium and the weathered sand-stone of these parts, but the other secret of the fertility of the place is the shelter from the north afforded by the Sidlaws. Pastures here are more lush, turnips fatter, crops turn golden earlier; and in modern times of course the wise farmer has turned to soft fruits which find a ready market in the Dundee jam factories. Tough as he may have been, however, the medieval laird was even more sensitive than we are to the advantages of favourable micro-climates, to use the jargon of our times, for he had not our means of bringing about easier cropping. Conse-quently the dells and dens along the south fringe of the Sidlaws are dominated by a succession of castles and noble houses of different periods. There are Kinfauns, facing across the river to the ruinous pile of Elcho, and Pitfour, Megginch, Fingask, Huntly, the Tower of Kinnaird. They are not among the most spectacular strongholds in the country, but they are good examples of "gentlemen's seats" of the fifteenth and sixteenth centuries, erected on their lands with due licence from the king.

At the east end of the Carse, on the higher ground between Inver-gowrie and the hills, is the little kirk of Fowlis Easter, the only place of worship in Scotland still decorated with pre-Reformation devotional paintings. How they escaped destruction is unexplained. As late as 1610 we find the synod decreeing "that the paintrie whilk is upon the pulpitt and ruid laft of Fowlis, being monuments of idolatry, sud be obliterated bi laying it over with green colour". Three years later things are still as they were, for in a letter to the synod the minister declares that "my Lord Gray will demolish such of the paintrie as is offensive". There are four works. They depict a Crucifixion scene, the Virgin Mary, the Baptist and St. Catherine. Originally, no doubt, all the walls were painted in similar style. It is unlikely, I think, that these paintings were imported from Flanders, as some have claimed, for there is enough *naiveté* in the treatment to indicate a native artist, though it is probable

61

enough he was one of the numerous Flemings whom trade brought over to the shores of Forth and Tay in the Middle Ages. The first church on the site is said to have been built in the twelfth century as the token of a lady's hope for her husband's safe return from the Crusades, but the oldest parts of the present church date from the mid-fifteenth century.

Prosaically now known as A.9, the Great North Road out of Perth is like a beckoning hand to all who visit the Highlands. It is the main route to Inverness and the far north, the only route which strikes with any sort of directness through the mass of the Grampians, so it has been the concern of engineers from General Wade in the eighteenth century onwards. Their most recent efforts have straightened so many of the bends and widened so many cuttings and tempered so many gradients that strangers seem more intent on finding how far on their way they can get before lunching than they are on discovering what lies along the road; but for anyone making Perth a centre for a few days it can be the path of some leisurely exploring.

The first stretch leads uneventfully enough across the upper portion of Strathmore. The plunge into the hills is made with dramatic suddenness: a few climbing curves of the road, a closing-in of trees, and within a few hundred yards the Tay which has appeared below us to the right is a fast, brown Highland river, and the woods to the left rise steep and dark with pines. Indeed, one may realise that these thick-set pines on their crags are the trees of Birnam Wood itself, that sinister wood which in Shakespeare's version of the story spelt the end of Macbeth. Another mile or two and the road swings across the Tay into the narrow main street of Dunkeld. It is all too easy to press on and miss the real Dunkeld, the sleepy precinct to the west and just beside the river. A threat to these delightful old houses seems to have been averted, and after the noise and smell of the heavy traffic in the High Street they form an appropriate introduction to the cathedral beyond. The cathedral church of St. Columba is one of the most beautiful ruins in Scotland, and it has been described as the most beautifully situated cathedral in Britain. Lawns, shaded by trees, reach up to its grey stones from the river's edge, a river here spanned by a bridge which Telford erected in 1809. The cathedral is long and narrow in the manner of Dunblane. Part of it, the aisleless choir, serves as the parish church of to-day, but the nave has been roofless and ruined since the Reformation. The choir is in fact the oldest portion of the building, much of it, including a fine arcade along the north wall, being thirteenth-century work, although there has been a great deal of reconstruction. The nave is fifteenth century. It is on record that even at this time there was no sort of road to the cathedral and mortar had to be carried in baskets and stones on the backs of horses. The tower is specially notable, its massive buttresses typically Scots. Dunkeld is a good example of the asymmetrical modifications of the Gothic style which the Scots tended to employ, avoiding that regularity which, as one writer has remarked, spoilt some of the finest work in France and England.

There are several tombs worth looking for. One of the finest, in the choir, shows a fully-armoured knight with the inscription: *Hic iacet Alexander Senescalus filius Roberti Regis Scotorum et Elizabeth Mare Dominus de Buchan et Dno de Badenoch qui abit vigesimo quarto die Julii.* The last eight words are restored. This would seem to be the resting place of that son of King Robert II who was known as the Wolf of Badenoch, a lawless character who carried fire and sword across the Highlands in the latter half of the fourteenth century, and whose name we will meet with again more than once. In the roofless nave is the grave of the last lineal descendant of the Young Pretender, Count Roehenstart, a son of Charlotte, Duchess of Albany, who died in 1854. Dunkeld had various associations with the Pretender, who sent Lochiel and Nairne to proclaim his father king as James VIII from the cross. The best of the surviving tombs however is in the south wall of St. Ninian's Chapel: a mitred bishop with his staff under a canopy. He is Bishop Cardeny, who began the building of the nave in 1406.

Dunkeld's importance as a religious centre goes back eleven centuries. When the raids of the northmen rendered Iona insecure, Kenneth MacAlpine transferred the relics of St. Columba from the western island to this pleasant spot among the hills, although it seems to have been a centre of both sacred and royal significance for centuries before this. The first part of the name certainly means an eminence or a fort, and the second part associates the place either with the Celts in general or with the Culdees, the Celtic Church, in particular.

Certainly with the coming of Columba's relics Dunkeld became the mother-church of Scotland. Even this secluded place among the hills was not beyond the reach of the Viking invaders. Their first attempt to reach it, under Ragner Lodbrog in 845, met with defeat near Clunie at the hands of MacAlpine himself with a combined force of Picts and Scots, but in 907 they captured and devastated it.

A few miles up Strathtay, at Ballinluig, the Tummel joins the Tay. By following the Tay, one may circle back and eventually return to Perth, a rewarding route in terms both of scenery and of historical associations. At this point where it is joined by the Tummel the Tay suddenly alters its course from one flowing with the general strike of the rocks to the channel which we have been following which breaks south-eastwards through the hill ranges. Not only does this lend the river some exceptional scenic effects, but it draws into it an immense drainage system, the outflow of an area of 2,750 square miles, bringing down a greater volume of water than any other British river. Small wonder no other excels it as a salmon stream.

Aberfeldy, some 10 or 12 miles up the Tay from its meeting with the Tummel, like Dunkeld was a centre both of the Picts and of the Culdees, but its chief visible link with the past now is the superb Tay Bridge. With wide central arch and approaches each with two arches, this is the best example of all the bridges which General Wade built to keep open military communications through the Highlands. Wade left his mark all over the Central Highlands. Despite the fact that he was commander of the army of occupation after the failure of the rising of the 'Fifteen, his work has linked his name with the Highland landscape, and his memory lingers in a kind of aura of beneficence. In contrast to the uncompromising Cumberland, Wade can almost be represented as the dupe of the people on whom he was supposed to be imposing military discipline. Instead of carrying out the disarming acts with the harshness which followed Culloden, Wade found himself receiver of vast contributions of rusty, obsolete weapons when the well-oiled dirks and broad-swords were being concealed in the thatch of their owners' houses, while as commander-in-chief of the Government forces opposed to Charles Edward he was quite bewildered by the elusiveness of the Jacobite army. If such weaknesses earn him the indulgence of

patriotic Scots, his work as a road and bridge builder turns the feeling
into something like affection.

> *Had you seen these roads before they were made*
> *You would lift up your hands and bless General Wade.*

For generations this tag was repeated in the Highlands, where the old
soldier completed 250 miles of metalled roads of a standard width of
16 feet, and the road making involved him in the building of 40 bridges,
ranging from monumental structures like Aberfeldy's Tay Bridge to
quite modest affairs, but all so soundly devised that some at least, Tay
Bridge being one, can carry the heavy motor traffic of to-day without
any strengthening. The task began in 1725, and the roads and bridges
were all completed by 1736. It was summer work only, and very
economical, for 500 soldiers were the labourers and they got only
sixpence a day in addition to their meagre pay. The resulting communications system, in spite of the forts and bases which supplemented
it, seems to have had very little effect on the course of the rebellion of
'Forty-five when it came; yet it helped to open up an almost impenetrable country.

Beside the bridge at Aberfeldy is another symbol of a new era in the
Highlands: the Black Watch memorial cairn. In this age when the
sentiments and traditions of famous Highland regiments seem to be at
a discount in quarters which should know better, it is perhaps good to
remember that on this spot beside the Tay in 1739 the first of these
regiments was embodied as a regiment of the line in the British Army.
It was of course all part of the attempt to put down and control the
Highland "savages"; but one must concede that even as late as the
beginning of the eighteenth century there were many among the clans
who made uncomfortable neighbours not only for the Lowlanders and
Sassenachs to the south but also for sober Highlanders like Duncan
Forbes of Culloden who felt it was time his countrymen ceased settling
disputes with the edge of the sword. The Freiceadan Dubh, the Black
Watch, got their name because their tartans were sombre by contrast
with the Saighdearn Dearg, the redcoats of the Regular Army. They
were raised in this region, and most of the recruits seem to have been
sons of tacksmen and landed families, picked for their stature and mien.
They seem to have thought their service was to be confined within

Scotland, and Forbes himself, then President of the Court of Session in Edinburgh, objected when the regiment was ordered to London. All went well until after a review on Finchley Common by General Wade these haughty gentlemen of the Black Watch realised that some of the Londoners regarded them as a comic spectacle. Jacobite agents put it about in the regiment that the march south was merely the first step towards exile in the plantations, and most of the regiment melted away only to be rounded up and tried for their lives as deserters. Three were actually executed, the rest dispersed among other regiments. It was an inauspicious start; but such battle honours did they accumulate within the next 75 years that when they came back from the Peninsular War the welcoming crowds in the streets of Edinburgh were so dense that the pipers could not play.

At Aberfeldy there are two tempting roads to choose from. One can proceed by Taymouth Castle, once the seat of Campbell of Glenorchy and now a Civil Defence college, to Loch Tay and the road which leads under the shadow of Ben Lawers, famed for its alpine flora, to Killin, returning to Perth by way of St. Fillans; or one may climb by the Strath of Appin over the hills and back to the Great North Road. The second alternative breaks more new ground. First it crosses the mouth of Glen Lyon. Fortingall, a few miles up this road, is worth a visit, though the site marked "Roman Camp" in maps is no such thing but the remains of a medieval moated fort. The strath road climbs round the base of Schiehallion, one of the most shapely hills in Scotland as its name is one of the most euphonious, and, joining the Kinloch Rannoch road, doubles back by Loch Tummel to join the Great North Road at the famous Pass of Killiecrankie.

In the days of the Highland Railway Killiecrankie was perhaps the most eagerly-awaited feature on the route. Noses of small boys and girls were pressed to windows almost before the train had left Pitlochry station, and eyes peered down through the hanging woods of the gorge to where the waters of the Garry swirled and foamed:

> *Horse and man went down like driftwood,*
> *When the floods are black at Yule;*
> *And their carcases are whirling*
> *In the Garry's deepest pool*

The spectacular scenery of the Pass has probably enhanced the Jacobite victory of 1689 here, a victory turned to disaster by the loss of the Jacobite leader, Dundee, in the first clash. The battle of Killiecrankie is the classic example of the Highlander's superiority over regular troops where the terrain is rugged and familiar. It also provides two object-lessons for the student of war weapons. In the first place it proved the futility of the old plug bayonet, which, in the face of an attacking enemy, had to be plugged into the gun muzzle after the piece had been discharged, wasting fatal moments. In the second, it illustrated the efficiency of the Highland broadsword in skilled hands.

This celebrated weapon, the broadsword, may be examined at leisure, and in variety, on the walls of Blair Castle, at Blair Atholl, a short distance north on the road from the Pass. It is called a broadsword because it is two-edged, as distinct from the single-edged backsword, and it is fitted with a massive basket hilt. The one thing it must never be called is a claymore, for the claymore is a two-hander even larger in size, as it name implies, and now exceedingly rare. The superb blades of the best broadswords were usually forged in Germany or in Spain, but the basket hilts were made in Scotland, some of the best of them at Stirling. There is a large and varied armoury of Highland weapons of all sorts at Blair, which is the seat of the Duke of Atholl. Old as some parts of the castle are—Cumming's Tower was built in the thirteenth century by Comyn of Badenoch—it is specially notable as a museum of Highland relics. Also it is one of the places redolent of the lavish hospitality typical of the Highlander even when it is far beyond his means. It was on the Atholl lands that that extraordinary entertainment took place which Scott describes in *Tales of a Grandfather*, when James V came hunting with a great retinue which included the Papal Legate and the Italian Ambassador. John, the third Earl, built for his guests in a quiet meadow a rustic palace with apartments filled with flowers, a wooden palace defended by wooden towers and surrounded by ponds stocked with succulent fish. To the astonishment of the Italians, the Highlanders burned the fantastic structure as the guests departed—an even more graceful and extravagant gesture than breaking glasses after a toast! Thirty-five years later, in 1564, Mary Queen of Scots was entertained at Blair. William Barclay, later Professor of Civil Law at Angers University, has left an account of a grand *battue* in which 2,000 clansmen drove the game in from Atholl, Badenoch, and even Mar and Moray. The final bag was 360 deer and 5 wolves. A number of relics still in the castle call to mind that the same spirit of generous entertainment persisted at the time of Queen Victoria's visit in 1844. Host and hostess greeted the Queen and her husband and the Princess Royal at their door and handed over the castle to them in its entirety for a three-week stay. The comment of the *Statistical Account*, that Blair may be said to be "one of the most splendid hunting châteaux in Europe", is no exaggeration.

CHAPTER FOUR

Brechin and Strathmore

Strathmore and the Howe of the Mearns and the lands bordering the mouth of the Firth of Tay were, as a region, probably explored more thoroughly by the Romans than they are by the average visitor to Scotland to-day. Thousands, of course, throng the coastal resorts every summer, Carnoustie has a place in the calendar of big golf, and Glamis is on the programme of the 'bus tours making for what they advertise as Royal Deeside; but this long, fertile strip bordering the Grampians is a tangle of by-ways which are full of interest if one is armed with a little information. I have chosen Brechin as the centre. It is a characteristic town, with good features of its own.

Brechin is on the long road that leads through Strathmore and on to Stonehaven and Aberdeen. It tends to follow the high ground on the north slope of the Sidlaws while it can. While it clings to the heights the views are superb. Thirty miles of green, wooded country stretch from south-west to north-east, veined with little watercourses and with roads, and dotted with farms and villages. This green prosperity on the far side of the strath changes to blue and grey and purple where the Grampian wall begins, and the wall is broken by the shadowed mouths of glens, many small but among them the longer, climbing glens of Shee and Isla, of Prosen and Clova and Esk. The great peaks are far away behind these foothills: it is 20 miles to Cairn of Claise and more to Lochnagar. But there is no difficulty in understanding why the Romans pressed on through the broad, safe lands of the strath, looking all the time over their shields at the glens in which they knew the enemy lurked.

The red sandstone on which Strathmore is founded is soft and has yielded up for the farmer a rich, red tilth which in spring is in fine contrast to the growth in the hedges; but it is not a very beautiful building stone, and a town like Brechin, which is built of it, at first has a rather grim look, especially on a grey day when the red in the stone does not come to life. Brechin, nevertheless, is a town of character. The nineteenth century, if it contributed nothing notable, at least built in the same material as the thirteenth, lending a sense of wholeness. The hub of the old town is the celebrated round tower, also of the red stone. This is one of the truly significant monuments of Scotland. Its solitary parallel in Scotland is the round tower of Abernethy, not far from Perth. These towers are matched only by the round towers of Ireland, built as refuges for the clergy in times of invasion by the Northmen, and the Scottish towers are reminders of our colonisation, both racial and religious, by the Irish. The Brechin tower has some specially interesting features. Windows and door have jambs not vertical but inclined towards one another, a form typically Celtic, and the carving of the Crucifixion above the door is quite foreign to our eyes, accustomed to Gothic forms, the legs of the Christ hanging uncrossed in the Irish way. The supporting priests, too, are of the Irish Church, one with the pastoral staff known as the *bachuill*, the other bearing a tau cross. The remoteness and loneliness of Celtic Christianity, cut off from Rome and the classical tradition by the barbarian mainland of Europe over a period of hundreds of years, can be read in these details of stonework. Two weird beasts guarding the door are also thoroughly Irish. The tower is in fact all that remains of a Culdee monastery, which was probably found on a spot hallowed formerly by the Picts, for it was a practice of the ancient church to modify tradition rather than break it. Hector Boece refers to a Danish invasion of Angus shortly after the year 1000, and states that Brechin was burned with the exception of "a certain round tower built with marvellous art".

The tower contrasts rather oddly with the cathedral beside it. It may have served as the steeple of the original cathedral, but the present structure had its beginning early in the thirteenth century, and the square tower to the north-west is the work mainly of Bishop Patrick, who held office from 1351 to 1383. At first sight the cathedral looks as English as the round tower is Irish, but there is a great deal of Scottish detail. There has been much reconstruction, and neither the ten altars nor any part of the original woodwork or stained glass remains. Indeed, in 1806 it was advocated that the round tower itself should be taken down to provide material for reconstruction, and it may only have been saved by the threat of Lord Panmure to hang the first man to lay a hand on it.

Strathmore is as liberally endowed with Pictish relics as the Western Highlands are with more generally familiar forms of Celtic monuments.

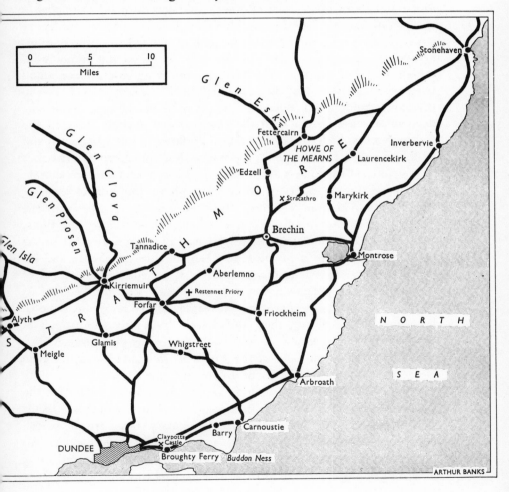

One might spend a long time quartering the countryside in search of them. An afternoon's excursion from Brechin, however, can take in quite a number of the more interesting relics, although there are many features other than Pictish to enliven the circuit and make the spending of a longer time worth while.

Making westwards from Brechin, the B-class road which branches left just outside the town and crosses the South Esk comes in a few miles to the village of Aberlemno. "Aber" is in itself a pointer to the Picts, and there used to be at Aberlemno several good examples of their stone carving, one or two of which have been removed. There are still two stones by the roadside, one of which has representations of figures, some on horses. The warriors, mounted and unmounted, carved in relief on the slab, before weathering might have stood comparison with some of the best ancient Chinese work, the horses in particular being most sensitive and spirited renderings, while the decorative sense shown is of the standard one expects from all the Celtic peoples. The road leads on into Forfar, and just a little way out of the town on the neighbouring road is Restennet Priory. This is a very significant monument. In several ways it appears to commemorate the conversion of the Picts from the Irish to the Roman form of Christianity. The climax of the celebrated *Ecclesiastical History* by the Venerable Bede is the chapter in which Nechtan, King of the Picts, asks Abbot Ceolfrid of Wearmouth to send him not only a list of the points of difference in practice between the Roman church and his own but also architects to make a church of stone after the manner of the Romans. St. Boniface was the missionary sent by Ceolfrid in response to Nechtan's appeal in the year 710. We know he came to Restennet. Is the priory, then, the church "built after the manner of the Romans"? The ruins as they exist are the ruins of a later, Augustinian house; but the base of the tower is undoubtedly earlier than Norman, the best evidence of this being the east archway with voussoirs which seem to belong to Saxon times. This could place the lower part of the tower safely in the eighth century, and it is difficult to avoid the exciting conclusion that these hoary stones are the bridge between two epochs in Scottish, and indeed British history. An interesting sidelight on this mission of Boniface's is a sculptured stone in a wall of the church at Invergowrie, across the Sidlaw hills from

Restennet. This is a little out of the circuit of Pictish monuments which I am concerned with, but the stone embodies as nothing else does the actual romanisation of Pictavia, for it shows three priests, clearly with the Roman form of tonsure of which Boniface makes so much, and with them two of those grotesque monsters which survived from the Picts' pre-Christian past. These priests may well have been members of Boniface's mission, for the stone must date from his time.

South-west of Forfar is the village of Glamis. It, too, comes into my Pictish pilgrimage. Down a lane off the twisting main road are the church and manse, and here too the Picts have left fragments behind them, and the manse has a stone on which the ancient, probably pagan facility for drawing horses has had grafted on to it a classical influence to produce a perfectly good centaur! This is much subtler evidence of conquest than anything the legions left behind them. There are many fragments of this type of stone-carving around: one, with some typically ·Celtic interlace, is even leaning against the door-jamb of Glamis church. And the district is still conscious enough of the tradition for local wood-carvers to have decorated the pew-ends in the church with motifs which at least show enough of the old feeling to aim at maximum variety.

One should pause in Glamis to look at more than Pictish relics. It is an attractive village built of a warm grey sandstone instead of the red so usual in Angus, and rather surprisingly so indifferent to tourists that there is not even a tea-shop in it. Its pleasantest corner is perhaps the lane that leads to the church, with its simple gardens and its background of superb trees—there is no county in the north which grows more splendid forest trees than Angus. The main feature of the lane now is the Angus Folk-Museum. It consists of a long row of old cottages run together to form one building, the front being simply decorated with quern-stones and similar things. The interior provides a long vista down the length of what used to be the series of cottages, an oddly impressive vista in spite of the narrow width and low roof. The museum is a storehouse of byegones relating to the county, ranging from spoons and samplers to a loom symbolic of the industry which supported so many of the towns and villages of Strathmore. The most ambitious exhibits are two rooms typical of Angus dwellings of perhaps a century ago. One is a simple cottage interior complete with box-beds, the other a more genteel room furnished with a variety of Victoriana. The nucleus of the collection was formed by Lady Maitland, but the enterprise is now carried on by a committee which is still adding valuable material as the older life of the district slowly disintegrates. There are two or three similar museums in Scotland, as we shall see; but the pity is that there is not one to every county, or region, for the amount of material being lost annually must be enormous.

The main feature of Glamis is the castle. It has of course added to its popular attraction in recent times because it was the childhood home of the Queen Mother, whose father was fourteenth Earl of Strathmore, but it is in many ways the epitome of the true Scottish castle before the impact of the Renaissance and classical ideas changed the nature of these great residences. It is typical, in the first place, in the relationship between the castle and its surroundings, for it grows straight out of the parklands like an enormous outcrop of rock instead of out of a contrived setting of avenues and gardens. The medieval structure no doubt was predominantly of a military nature, and the main surviving portion of this is the central tower; but the greater part of the castle as it exists was reconstructed at the beginning of the seventeenth century by Patrick, Lord Glamis, who became first Earl of Kinghorne, and he succeeded in changing what may have been a grim enough fortress into a home of great charm. His successors, too, took much delight in developing the castle. Indeed the third Earl, who became Earl of Strathmore in 1672, kept a record of his work in the Book of Record, a manuscript which he wrote himself and which has been a mine of information for historians and writers of after times. Perhaps the most delightful feature of the Record is his repeated apologies for not having recourse to a "public architect" in designing what he calls his "reformations". He says that "the not-seeking and taking counsell is commonly the cause why things are found amiss in the most part of men's doeings in that way; nor have I the vanity to consider my owne judgement as such as another cannot better." But it is this natural growth, this organic quality, which makes these northern castles of the seventeenth century what they are. A turret here, a corbelled-out corner there: these things reflect the life of the men and women living inside, reflect the requirements of generation after generation so that the building acquires character as an ageing face does, and with it the same sort of beauty. This, perhaps, is where these castellated Scottish structures are more appealing than the much grander French *châteaux* from which they borrow so many of their characteristics. There is no more visible aspect of the old alliance between France and Scotland than the clustered turrets of the castles in the two countries; but, as the third Earl of Strathmore would have said, the French turrets are contrived, the Scottish added more "to please and divert . . . than out of any ostentations."

The new spirit in castle-building is finely expressed in the Great Hall at Glamis. Here we have a barrel-vaulted medieval hall, that rather comfortless centre of baronial life, converted to a drawing-room which almost anticipates the elegance of the eighteenth century. Its crowning glory is the plaster ceiling with moulded ribs and pendants, dated 1621. It is the work of an English plaster-worker who has some other fine ceilings to his credit up in Aberdeenshire, notably at Craigievar. The huge Renaissance fireplace is equally good, above it the monogram of the second Earl and his wife, Margaret Erskine. His son has recorded his pride in and affection for this chamber. A family-group painting of him hangs high on an end wall, presiding over a room which he must have done much to make as it is to-day, for the furnishings belong to his time at the earliest. He completed his university education at St. Andrews in the year of the Restoration, and had to set about a private restoration of his own in the castle, which appears to have been stripped of its fineries and furnishings in the Royalist cause. Inevitably, he had to employ a good many visiting craftsmen. Among them was the Dutchman, Jacob de Wett, fresh from the marathon contract for the portraits of Scottish kings which still hang in the long gallery of the Palace of Holyroodhouse in Edinburgh. De Wett's Glamis work, in the chapel, is much more pleasing.

The procession of distinguished visitors who have passed through Glamis, staying there briefly, is endless. It includes many historical figures, among them leading protagonists on both sides in the Jacobite risings, although the "Butcher" Cumberland was no welcome guest. The procession includes also some eminent literary men, who have left some record of their impressions. Gray in 1765 was carried away by the vision of its clustered towers, and Scott a generation later, equally impressed, was stirred by a kind of superstitious awe.

The Pictish pilgrimage takes us west for 10 or 12 miles along the high road to Meigle. Meigle stands on a cross-roads and must have done for many hundreds of years, for it is a tangle of the tracks of history. The Roman legions made one of these tracks, for they camped at Cardean, to the north of Meigle, in A.D. 84. It must have been a Pictish centre, however, long before this, as well as long after. Few places have furnished so much solid evidence of Pictish culture. The sculptured stones of Meigle have provided us with an extraordinarily baffling picture of pagan, classical and Christian elements blended in Pictish art. Daniel has been depicted in the lions' den done, as one writer has pointed out, in the manner of the catacombs, and we find here, too, the square, squat cross carved in relief, typical of the Pictish north-east as the free-standing Iona form of cross is typical of the western seaboard. But associated with these Christian symbols are the usual skilfully-drawn animals and monsters, and with them centaurs and swastika-like knots of naked human forms which seem to reflect the influence of the classical art of the Mediterranean. Seekers after ancient relics in this little wayside churchyard may, incidentally, be surprised to find there the grave of Sir Henry Campbell-Bannerman, the one-time prime minister, whose family home of Stracathro is on the other side of Brechin.

Stracathro borders on the Howe of the Mearns, a district worth exploring in a leisurely way. It is the country of the brilliant novels of Lewis Grassic Gibbon, the gaunt, earthy quality of which is in such contrast to the plays of that son of nearby Kirriemuir, Sir James Barrie. But there is nothing gaunt about the countryside of the Howe of the Mearns. Its villages and its wooded roads, with glimpses of the Grampian skyline, place it among the most unspoilt parts of Scotland. Two of its principal villages are alike in being approached through a kind of triumphant archway built of the local red sandstone to span the main road. Of the two, Fettercairn is the more attractive in itself; but the more interesting historically is Edzell, although the straight, wide, pleasant street of modern houses and hotels gives no hint of this. The interest lies in the castle. Or perhaps it should be said, in the garden of the castle, for this is one of the earliest surviving pleasaunces in Scotland, and to pass through Edzell on a fine summer day in ignorance of this delightful place only a short distance up the side road

13   The Howe of the Mearns, Kincardineshire

to the north of the village would be a great shame. It is well known that the Scots are a race of gardeners, but there are those who think the Scots did their gardening in England, and there are others, who know a little better, who are under the impression such improvements and amenities belong to the eighteenth century. In fact, pleasure gardens of this kind were in being in early sixteenth-century Scotland, but little remains of them; and although not much survives of the original pleasaunce at Edzell except the walls and the garden house, the Ministry of Works has done much to recover its attraction by filling it with flowers. The characteristic "big house" garden in Scotland is usually, as at Edzell, surrounded by a wall. This provides a microclimate which has favoured some amazing achievements, and peaches have been induced to ripen regularly and exotics to bloom long before the advantages of glass were exploited. The ninth Earl Crawford enlarged the castle itself at the end of the sixteenth century, but it is his son, Sir David Lindsay, who made the garden in 1604. The garden is of architectural as well as horticultural interest; but its most important single feature is the series of stone sculptures on the walls, heraldic decorations, among them panels depicting the virtues, the liberal arts and the planetary deities. These have been identified as copies of a series of copperplate engravings usually attributed to Georg Pencz of Nuremberg, a pupil of Dürer himself. Sir David Lindsay, Lord Edzell, is known to have visited Nuremberg, for he brought two mining engineers with him from that city, with the idea of their helping him to look for precious metals up Glenesk, in the hills behind Edzell.

The workings at the head of Glenesk are said to be traceable still, but the best reward for the journey up that long but lovely glen is a visit to the tiny Glenesk Folk-Museum at Tarfside, creation of the schoolmistress, Miss Michie, especially rewarding if the excellent institution of home-baked teas there continues. The museum is limited to byegones of Glenesk itself, and it has no spectacular exhibits, but it is an extraordinary documentary record of the life of a very small community.

Mention of byegones is a reminder that the neighbouring town of Laurencekirk, strung out along the main road five miles from Fettercairn, was once renowned for the manufacture of some of the most

79

14   Eilean Donan Castle, Ross and Cromarty

pleasing snuff-boxes which have come down to us from the past. They may seem modest beside those gold-and-enamel boxes carried by gentlemen at the court of Louis XVI; but in their way they are just as finely made, and they reflect a way of life quite as perfectly. They are entirely of wood: indeed, in this and their other features they are exceedingly difficult to distinguish from the boxes made in the village of Mauchline in Ayrshire at about the same time. They are, however, as delicately constructed as a Japanese trinket, and their characteristic feature is the ingenious roll-hinge, working on a wooden pin, so snug that it is hard to see how it was made. Sometimes the sheer beauty of the wood is decoration enough, more often a pattern or a picture is drawn or painted on the exterior and protected by a translucent varnish of great purity. More than one firm made these boxes, but chief among them was Charles Stiven and Son, the Christian name of the founder of which was bestowed in memory of Charles Edward himself. They were Jacobite supporters, the Stivens, and their zeal for the cause is reflected in some of their boxes. It was a great snuff-consuming district. Lord Gardenstone was laird, and he himself was a patron of much worth, for he used to say that if he had a dozen noses he would willingly supply them all with snuff. He is said to have been so lavish with the stuff that the folds of his waistcoat were filled with it, and the villagers helped themselves when talking to him. He was a patron of Stiven, whose establishment survived his rivals' and was eventually appointed Box-maker to Her Majesty. Indeed, the head of the firm himself took his boxes for inspection to Balmoral on the other side of the hills. These beautiful little boxes are becoming rarer every year, and it is hard to come by a good one in the antique shops except at a stiff price. Very often the name of the maker can be found stamped inside the lid. The Stivens, although it is not generally known, had more than a luxury trade. They made a variety of small wooden goods, among them that once-popular toy now known by its name alone: the teetotum. The teetotum was a cube with a stalk on which it could be spun by a twirl of finger and thumb, and "Stiven's totums" were highly popular with the 'teenagers of a century and more ago, priced at one halfpenny. The stakes in this gambling game, in the Howe of the Mearns at least, were nothing more deadly than a Yule preen or nut.

Brechin is within easy reach of the coast. The Angus coastline is perhaps the least highland feature of the region which, for the purpose of this book, has been called the Highlands. Inland, the sandstone has weathered down into good farming land which slopes gently seawards, but it affords small shelter from the east winds which, for long periods, especially during spring and early summer, blow with a grim, grey persistence off the grey North Sea which rims all the eastern horizon. I once worked on a farm in these parts, and I can still recall the search-ing chill of the haars, those streaming wet sea-mists which are the curse of so much of the Scottish east coast. They crept up the bare, furrowed fields where we were "clatting the neeps" and made one think of the welcome shelter of the stackyard and even the comfort of standing with sack-bound legs in a steaming, aromatic midden in the lee of a hedge! But the sea-coast itself produces unexpected amenities: fine beaches and noble dunes, superbly-turfed links of the kind which have made Scotland the natural home of golf.

Arbroath is, historically speaking at least, the most notable of the coastal towns. The way to it lies through a village with the strange name of Friockheim, pronounced Froohy. Strathmore and Angus are unusually rich in odd names: Whigstreet, Clocksbriggs, Carrot, Tigerton, Phesdo, Monboddo and many more. They have, too, a habit of quaintly linking names, as for example, Kirkton of Kingoldrum, Kirkton of Menmuir, Brown Cathertun, Bridgend of Lintrathen. This Lowland, almost Sassenach feeling in the place-names extends far up into the hills behind Strathmore, so that even at the 3,000-foot watershed one finds Mount Keen and Braid Cairn, which might belong in the Lammermuirs or the Pentlands, shouldering the vast hinterland of Gaelic bens. Arbroath is solidly an Angus town, even to the rather grim red sandstone of which it is built. By origin it was no doubt an ecclesiastical settlement. The abbey is a twelfth-century foundation; and at the equally old church of St. Vigean's just outside the town there are sculptured stones, as in so many parts of Strathmore and Angus, which point to Pictish occupation. The abbey is now the core of interest in Arbroath. It is unique in Scotland in that it is dedicated to St. Thomas à Becket, and the dedication was made by William the Lion in 1173, two years after the death of the saint at Canterbury. It may seem strange that a Scots king should have done such a thing, but apparently it was William's medieval way of expressing in a durable form his feelings about Henry II of England. It was a Benedictine house, and the monks were brought from Kelso. The abbey is now in ruins, but even in this state it is impressive. Although like most Scottish abbeys it is not large by Continental standards the interior must have been rather splendid, if only because of the light effects, for the great rose window known as the Arbroath O and the arrangements to illuminate the altar at the east end must have dyed the rosy stonework in still richer colours. The foundation was well endowed with rights and privileges, its revenues coming from great land-holdings in the district, from profits from the harbour built by the monks, and from commercial privileges throughout the kingdom. Arbroath Abbey's historical fame, however, rests chiefly on its having been the scene of the signing of Scotland's counterpart to Magna Carta, the celebrated Declaration of Arbroath. This is one of the most remarkable documents in the history of democracy. Signed by King Robert the Bruce himself in the Regality Chamber of the Abbey, it called upon the Pope in ringing phrases to recognise the Scottish claim to independence and freedom; but the most remarkable part of it is the statement that the Scots will cast out their King himself, whose signature is on the parchment, should he betray them to the English. In brief, the greatest of Scotland's kings here signed and sealed an admission that in Scotland kings held office by no divine right, and he did it in 1320, three centuries before Charles I lost his head for trying to cling to such a divine right in England.

It is a straight run through the lowest of lowlands from Arbroath to the city of Dundee. The only natural feature of note on the way is the great group of golden sand dunes at Barry and Buddon Ness, the ultimate breakdown of the Old Red Sandstone of this region assailed by wind and water. Barry links are a miniature Scottish version of Salisbury Plain and many a Scot has endured camp life in this exposed wilderness of bent grass and natural bunkers, so easily adapted for the purposes of championship golf at neighbouring Carnoustie.

Dundee itself scarcely seems to fit into the general pattern of this book. There is no historic old town, little in the way of gracious or elegant buildings apart from the Caird Hall and one or two churches. Yet in its people and its story it is a city of immense character. It is the third city in Scotland, a city of nearly 200,000, the second in point of industrial output. It was in the forefront of the Reformation, solidly behind the martyred George Wishart; William Wallace was at school there; Hector Boece, one of the first and greatest recorders of Scottish history, was born there.

Only fragments of Dundee's past have survived. The most celebrated of them is the Old Steeple, overlooking the City Square, a really fine piece of fifteenth-century Gothic, somehow curiously Scottish in its blend of ecclesiastical with military architecture. Not that it was intended as a fortress, but it was actually used as a strong point in 1651, when a garrison defied the soldiers of General Monk until smoked out by them. It forms part of a group called the City Churches, but the four old churches comprising this were destroyed by fire in the nineteenth century and rebuilt. Unfortunately, destruction of old Dundee was not all accidental. A case in point is the old Town House built by William Adam in 1734, replaced by a modern building in 1932. The real record of Dundee's past achievements is to be seen in its waterfront, its shipyards, its factories and warehouses. Strictly speaking, we are not concerned with the industrial picture in this book; but there may be more interest, more nobility, in a labourer's wrinkled face than in an old warrior's, and the story of Dundee's commerce is as much an epic as the stories of the castles in Strathmore. The street called Seagate is now far back from the shore it must once have looked down on, and there are five miles of reclaimed land along the front on which streets and docks and all the railways in the city have been built. This work has been accomplished in the century and a half since 1793. It is the lasting monument to many phases of the city's prosperity: to the day when Dundee was one of the great gateways to the Continent, when even the wines of France and the Rhine came this way; to the day when the whalers swarmed here from the Arctic and Antarctic grounds; to the long-lasting link between Dundee and Calcutta, when the jute-ships plied and the sons of city merchants regularly did their time in India to learn about the source and nature of the raw material on which their great wealth depended. Even the big jam industry has its epic quality, if we remember it is based, or was originally, on the fertile soils and sheltered fields of the fruit farms of the Carse and

Blairgowrie. There are new industries in plenty now in Dundee, set in much handsomer surroundings than the old, but they do not seem likely to attain the grand stature of the jute men or the whalers.

The fringes of the city have more ancient remains than Dundee itself. I have already mentioned the remarkable stone at Invergowrie, four miles out on the Perth road. For the rest, I will call attention only to a strange building just beside the eastern approach to the city, at what is now the dormitory suburb of Broughty Ferry. It is the castle of Claypotts, inscribed with the two dates 1569 and 1588, between which it was probably built. Its strangeness is due to the imposition of domestic buildings on a fortress tower, so that it is a half-way house between a military structure and the splendid vernacular castles which followed it in time. Once it was the home of Graham of Claverhouse, and its squat, forbidding outline on a grey day looks appropriate to "Bloody Clavers".

CHAPTER FIVE

Aboyne and Deeside

The mass of mountain country which stretches from the Cairngorms eastwards to within a short distance of the sea, the better part of 100 miles, is crossed by only three roads. The first and longest joins Blairgowrie and Braemar, and at the summit of it is the notorious Devil's Elbow. Far to the east, and much shorter, are the Cairn o' Mounth and the Slug roads. From Brechin to the north the obvious choice is the Cairn o' Mounth, which climbs rapidly from Fettercairn into the Kincardineshire hills. Less testing than the Devil's Elbow, it provides nevertheless some miles of views of magnificent wild country, especially westwards over the Forest of Birse. "Forest", in the Highlands of Scotland, it is probably unnecessary to say, is an expanse of hill and glen which may possess few trees or none at all, and the prospect from the Cairn o' Mounth is one of rank upon rank of rolling blue hills to the horizon.

As soon as the road winds down to the Water of Feugh and the valley of the Dee one is aware of the subtle change. Although the moors give place to cultivation again, this country is quite unlike the Howe of the Mearns on the other side of the hills. Streams flow more clearly, more swiftly, stones of cottage and dyke and natural outcrop have a washed hardness and brightness, the air itself at most times of the year has a sharp and yet heady quality, often aromatic with the faint scent of moor plants or ferns or pine woods. There are moor plants and ferns and pine woods south of the hills too, but somehow their presence is less pervasive. We have, in fact, crossed a frontier: we are in the north.

Deeside merits a short chapter to itself because it is not quite like anywhere else in the Highlands. Like some of those Swiss valleys so cut off that life goes on very much as it has done for hundreds of years, the valley of the Dee is sufficiently protected from through traffic to preserve its identity. Of course, every summer it receives vast numbers of tourists from all over the world, but on the whole they respect it, and in any case they confine themselves to a few resorts. Deeside is, in a sense, a museum; and like most large museums it keeps some of its most interesting exhibits in corners where they have to be searched out. Deeside is a sort of glorious folk museum founded about a century ago by an enthusiast with great personal power and influence. In it, the genuinely old is blended with a romantic new concept of the past, but the result has every appearance of a going concern, and there is a bloom of prosperity over the valley from end to end which might be envied by statistically richer regions in the south. There are no great industries here except the tourist industry, and agriculture is on a very modest scale; but fields are trim, the woods well cared for, houses neat and solidly built, and even among the people one gets the feeling of being on the estate of a prosperous landed proprietor.

Aboyne is as good a centre as any for the Dee valley. It is not rich in the character and sort of features found in the other centres which we have chosen up to now, but it is a typical Deeside village: solid-built, well kept and cared for, beautifully situated close to a great loop of the river among splendid pine woods. It is not itself in the shadow of great hills, and the fact that the valley is comparatively open here means that there are more lateral routes to explore than there are in the villages further up the river.

Deeside is pre-eminently the country of "Scots Baronial". This is a phrase which should be applicable to any castellated structure in Scotland dwelt in by a baron at any time, but normally it applies to the great houses of the sixteenth and seventeenth centuries, in which Renaissance elements from the Continent are brilliantly married to the vernacular style, and to the great crop of Victorian imitations or adaptations.

Aboyne is admirably placed for visiting a group of the Renaissance houses which includes some of the finest there are. It consists of the castles of Midmar, Fraser, Craigievar, Cluny and Crathes. There is no better example than the last, Crathes. It embodies most of the features of the style, its setting is typical, it is the seat of a very old family and, not least among its advantages for the visitor, it is now the property of the National Trust for Scotland and so open for inspection at regular, stated times. Seen from the garden below, with a stone staircase climbing towards it between dark yews, Crathes Castle is perhaps the choicest thing of its kind in all Scotland. The late-sixteenth century tower, severely plain for most of its height, in its topmost third bursts into bartisans and towers and finally chimney-stacks intricately knit

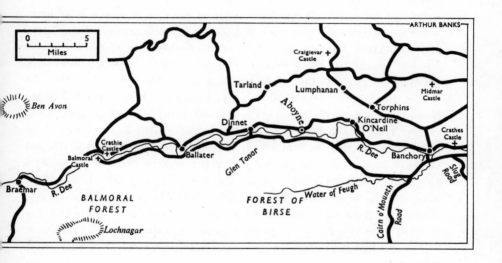

together by detail of corbelling and crowsteps and absurd, bristling little stone cannon in place of gargoyles. The stone detail is beautifully offset by the texture of the harled walls, that lime rendering of the stone walls applied perhaps mainly for its waterproofing qualities but which has a characteristic aesthetic appeal of its own. There is a remarkable unity about Crathes. It may reflect the continuity of occupation by the same distinguished family, the Burnetts of Leys. Originally Burnards, they were of Saxon stock and actually came to Scotland from Bedfordshire before the Norman conquest, a pedigree very unusual north of the Border. Alexander Burnard supported the Bruce in his bid for the throne, and it was in return for this that he received the lands on Deeside. A confirmation of his charter rights issued in 1358 is still shown in the castle. The family did not come to build at Crathes for another two centuries and the house, which took 40 years to build, was completed in 1596. The place was much improved by Thomas, first Baronet of Leys. Then came a long succession of distinguished lawyers and churchmen. Sir Thomas's brother was raised to the bench as Lord Crimond, and his son, Gilbert, entered the Church and went into exile in Holland with Charles II but became a friend of William of Orange, so that in 1688 he became Bishop of Salisbury and Chancellor of the Order of the Garter. His son William went to America and in course of time became Governor of New York, then of Massachusetts and of New Hampshire. A Gilbert Burnett became one of the most eminent Protestant philosophers of his time, holding the chair in this subject first at Basle, then at Montauban. At home, the James Burnett who was raised to the bench as Lord Monboddo was among the group of Scotland's most learned judges.

The Trust has taken over Crathes complete with its furnishings and heirlooms, so that it is as much the perfect example of a Highland castle of its period inside as outside. It is complete even to the ancient Horn of Leys, which hangs above the mantelpiece in the Great Hall, although the horn itself does not form part of the gift to the Trust. Alexander Burnard is said to have been given it, as a symbol of his tenure, from the Bruce when he handed over the lands of Crathes in 1323. The hall at Crathes is more characteristic than the hall at Glamis, with its rough stone-vaulted roof and window embrasures, but it too has lost its medieval air by accumulating an assortment of more comfortable furnishings from later ages. One medieval feature which it shares with Glamis, however, is the listening-hole near the door commonly known as the Laird's Lug, as it was intended to overhear talk of disaffection among the servants or of criticism among the guests. A finer room in some respects is the Long Gallery which spans the entire width of the building. Its ceiling is the original one of oak, with central bosses carved with the Royal Arms in token of the dispensation of justice which was one of the obligations of the laird as a tenant-in-chief. Indeed, it was in this room that the barony courts were held. But the ceiling for which Crathes is most noted is in the Chamber of the Nine Nobles, characters from the medieval minstrels' repertoire depicted on the boards above one's head. They are executed in tempera in a style once very common in Scotland and fortunately surviving in quite a number of great houses, and there is no finer example than this at Crathes. These ceilings appear to be native Scottish work without much question, unlike much of the better wood-carving. Closely examined they are naïve to the point of being comical, and by Continental standards crudely executed; but like many types of Scottish decorative art they are, in spite of their shortcomings, extraordinarily effective and pleasing in their general appearance. Many of the ceilings have been covered for centuries by plaster and rediscovered recently, so that the colours are astonishingly vivid. This Crathes ceiling carries the date 1602, and was rediscovered in 1877. In the room known as the Green Lady's Room there is another painted ceiling, but a less impressive one. The Green Lady is a ghost reputed to walk here with a child in her arms, and the tale was at least given some substance when men repairing the fireplace about a century ago found the skeleton of a child.

The gardens at Crathes are famous. It is perhaps not within the scope of a book about the Highlands to describe what individual gardeners, or even generations of gardeners, have contrived there; but there is a prevalent belief outside of Scotland that the only thing which blooms in the Highlands is the heather, and it is worth while pointing out that there are many places in the Highlands much better suited to good gardening than is the unsheltered, open country far to the south. It is true that in the early days gardening was despised by the Highlander, and that when the Grant clan took to making kitchen gardens after the 'Forty-five they were for a long time referred to as "the soft, kail-eating Grants". But fertile nooks in the shelter of the high hills are ideal for gardening, and the most astonishing plants and trees can be cultivated even in the eastern half of the country which, though less favoured in winter than the western seaboard, gets more sunshine in the summer. Crathes gardens date from the early eighteenth century, their yew hedges having been planted in 1702. Their deep, rich soil and fine aspect have made it possible to cultivate plants from China and India, from South America and New Zealand.

I will not describe the other castles in the so-called Midmar group, but all are well worth visiting. Midmar itself belongs to the Gordons of Cluny. George Bell, the master-mason probably responsible for it, is buried in Midmar churchyard under a stone dated 1575. Castle Fraser was built by another Bell, for he actually signed his work on a stone on the north front and dated it 1617. It has been called the most spectacular of the group. If so, Craigievar is perhaps the most beautiful. The colours of its walls and roofs are soft and warm. One of the Bell family no doubt built it too. Mr. Stewart Cruden in his *The Scottish Castle* says that Craigievar "as a work of art claims a Scottish place in the front rank of European architecture", and that its front elevations have "a sort of sublimity". He describes it as the apotheosis of its type. Nothing has been altered or added since it was built in 1626, and it has been continuously occupied.

From Aboyne westwards, Deeside has an indefinable air of being a great private estate. In spite of the grand sweep of the valley and the peaks of hills ringing the horizon, there is a well-kept look about the roads and fences, the fields and the plantations, which contrasts with the untamed moorlands of the north-west. One has a sense of rolling back the years at least to Edwardian times. The fact that the road leads nowhere except to high moors means there is little of the industrial traffic, few of the six-wheeled diesel lorries polluting the air, of the Great North Road in rival Speyside. It is true that horse-brakes have been replaced by shooting-brakes and that landed gentlemen move around in conveyances very much like anyone else's, as a rule; but somehow on Deeside that spirit of another age lingers, and August still means house-parties, rather than caravan sites.

In the main, of course, this is due to the Royal estates which do so much to determine the character of upper Deeside. Sixty years and more after, it is astonishing how the joys and, still more, the sorrows of the old Queen, linger in this place. The most concentrated evidence of it is in the church of Crathie, bowered in trees above the road where this makes a great bend around Balmoral. The church dates only from 1895, but it is well worth an hour, for its granite walls encompass an epoch. Here in a sense is the heart and core of "Balmoralism", that extraordinary cult which Queen Victoria created in this valley 100 years ago, and the influence of which on the whole of the Highlands is not yet dead. Not even the Taj Mahal is a more remarkable symbol of a passionate love for a dead partner. The Taj is glorious and perfect, but

15 The Dee near Braemar, Aberdeenshire

finite, whereas the memories of the old Queen were translated into a way of life which ended up by having a substantial influence on Scotland's social and economic systems. I said in the first chapter that she established a feudal matriarchy and won the sympathy of the Celt; but she also succeeded in changing the attitude of the outside world towards him, until men who had never set foot in the Highlands diligently sought for some shred of right to wear the tartan, that garb of the Gael which Continental propaganda in the time of Gustavus Adolphus had pointed at as the brand of barbarism, and which had actually been proscribed as treasonable less than a century before the Queen was crowned. Here in Crathie Church is the most intimate sight of the bond which grew between the widowed Queen and those she liked to think of as her fellow-parishioners. In this little parish church by the roadside there are memorials to sovereign after sovereign. Beside them are memorials to the men and women up and down the valley. Some of them were well known and loved in the Royal circle, for instance William Blair, whose stone is in the churchyard, "house carpenter and violinist", as he is described, but once known as the Queen's fiddler, one of a long line of Crathie musicians which goes back to John Bruce, who was said by Burns to have claimed the authorship of "O, whistle and I'll come to ye, my lad." And there is, of course, the memorial stone raised by the Queen herself to the memory of John Brown, "personal attendant and beloved friend", as she says of him on the stone. He was born at Crathienaird and died at Windsor.

Balmoral Castle itself is a notable example of the mode of building adopted by the new landlords of the Victorian age. To shrug off the style as of no architectural consequence, as most critics do to-day, is a confession of pedantry. Any style which perfectly reflects a way of life is of consequence. The strange proportions, the unsympathetic textures, the pompous exteriors, the cavernous kitchen quarters and chill stone passages—these things are as worthy of study as medieval barbicans and gatehouses. They are symptoms of a different sort of arrogance, of a different sort of contempt for discomfort. There is quality in the building of them. In a curious kind of way, they belong where they are. If their solecisms cause shudders, at least they are committed in no uncertain way, and often they betray the laudable enthusiasm of the amateur, as in the case of Balmoral, designed largely by no less an

16 Lochnagar and the Brig o' Dee, Aberdeenshire

architect than the Prince Consort himself, if the actual plans were prepared by the City Architect of Aberdeen.

Balmoral estate was at one time a possession of the earldom of Mar, which lost it in the forfeitures following upon the 'Fifteen rebellion; and the Farquharsons of Inverey, who had the freehold, lost this in the 'Forty-five. The Earl of Fife was the next owner. It was in 1847 that the Prince Consort leased the property, and he bought it a few years after. The present castle was built between 1853 and 1856. The Prince lived to enjoy it only for a few short years, but they were long enough for the Queen in his constant company to develop a deep attachment to the place, and the national memorial erected to his memory in Kensington is a piece of empty formality when compared with the cairn on the summit of Creag an Lurachain, the inscription on a stone of which carries complete conviction in spite of its hyperbole.

Where the Clunie Water joins the Dee in the shadow of Lochnagar is Braemar. Braemar is at a meeting of ways across the hills. The Devil's-Elbow road comes down here to Deeside, and here too begin the path to the Atholl country through the long, straight reach of Glen Tilt and the road which follows the Dee itself to its source in the Lairig Ghru, between Ben Macdhui and the precipices of the Garbh Corrie of Braeriach. Braemar has a place in history from very early times, but there is little to show for it. There are traces of Kindrochit Castle, hunting lodge of Robert I in the fourteenth century, which is responsible for the village's full name of the Castletown of Braemar, but for the past century the Invercauld Arms Hotel has covered the spot where the thirty-ninth Earl raised his standard on the Braes of Mar to launch the rebellion of 1715, and it must be recorded that the present Braemar Castle was built by the Government after the 'Forty-five as a barracks for troops sent to keep the clans in check.

It is near this castle that the most celebrated of all Highland gatherings is held annually, in August. In its present form the gathering dates back to about the beginning of Queen Victoria's reign, and so itself might almost be claimed as a feature of the legend of Balmoral; but there are other legends about the gathering's antiquity. One of them credits Malcolm Canmore with its foundation, holding that he offered a purse of gold to the fighting-man who, fully equipped, first reached the summit of Creag Choinnich. This tale at least points the moral of the true gathering, with its emphasis on toughness and endurance, and that the ending of this race up the Creag was apparently due to Victoria's displeasure is significant of the change of purpose in these events. Caber-tossing is still, perhaps, the climax of the typical gathering, with its premium on a nice mixture of might and skill, but there is a tendency for some gatherings to degenerate into mere athletic meetings, running strip and all. At Braemar the gathering is predominantly a great Highland event. The Royal Highland Society keeps a jealous eye on its standards. It has frowned, for example, on the practice of women and girls dancing in kilts, a practice which makes a mockery of so many minor so-called "Highland" gatherings both in Scotland and in the Commonwealth overseas. The kilt is a magnificent dress, but it is an exclusively male dress and so utterly unsuited to the female figure that no discriminating young woman would put it on in public; and when the whole is turned into a caricature of Highland regimentals complete with rows of tinkling medals the result is cheap and nasty enough to bring a blush of shame to any Highlander's cheek. The same is true of the spectacle of small girls engaging in the sword dance, so essentially the war dance of the fighting man, like the Maori *haka*, and when the little warrioresses trip around in their ballet-pumps between the crossed blades of a couple of English regimental dress swords supplied by a theatrical agency the last insult is added to the injured memory of past glories. The Aboyne authorities have laid down the correct garb for women dancers as a simple dress worn with the appropriate tartan shawl or sash, and the better gatherings have followed this example. The Highland gathering is a man's affair, from the lusty piping contest to the dignified presence of the clan chiefs with tall eagle-feathers in their bonnets.

CHAPTER SIX

Aberdeen and Buchan

In the region designated here as the Highlands, the only cathedral and university city is Aberdeen. Aberdeen is a coastal city and port, at a considerable distance even from the foothills of the Grampians, and it is inhabited by a dour, hard-headed breed of men without any trace of the Celtic temperament. The extraordinary thing is that Aberdeen nevertheless fits quite comfortably into the Highland picture. There is nothing incongruous about dealing with it in this Highland context.

Part of the explanation may lie in the material Aberdeen is made of. It has no backdrop of craggy mountains, but it is built on, and of, the material of those mountains. To understand this adequately one must go out to Rubislaw and gaze down into what must be one of the largest man-made holes in the world. The Rubislaw quarry has, in a sort of reverse sense, all the grandeur of a group of great buildings. Where the buildings soar to the light, it plunges deep into the shadows with a dramatic effect few buildings could match. The New York skyline is nothing to it, except perhaps when seen from the Hell-Gate Bridge against an angry sunset. Rubislaw is the work not of a few years but of centuries. Out of its bowels have come not merely the buildings which, from the Middle Ages to the present, have grown into Aberdeen, but to some extent too the character of the Aberdonians, tempered by their struggle with the sea and this enduring building material. It is granite, the material of the Grampians themselves, and because of this Aberdeen has some of the nature of Lochnagar, especially on a day of sun and rain, when her steeples and pinnacles by turns gloom and glitter against an inky sea and sky. Perhaps one day its Art Gallery, which already possesses one of the best little public collections of contemporary

British paintings, might commission John Piper to paint Rubislaw for its walls.

The historic core of the city is Old Aberdeen, separate from the rest of the city until incorporated in 1891, and the core of Old Aberdeen is the cathedral of St. Machar's. It, too, is built of granite: it is the only granite cathedral in Britain. It is in part the material no doubt which gives it its uncompromising, militant appearance, and the almost fortress-like west front at first sight seems determined by this. It is not quite like any other church, even in Scotland; and yet it is very Scottish. One of its finest features is the great west window, composed of seven tall, narrow lights with trefoil heads. The flanking towers have machicolated parapets, and slot windows only, like castles. Bishop Elphinstone completed a great central tower early in the sixteenth century, but in 1688 it was robbed of its buttresses to build a barracks and it fell down, to the detriment of what must have been a very impressive structure. It is still impressive, far beyond its actual scale. The surviving portion dates mainly from the fifteenth and sixteenth centuries; but maybe its most remarkable surviving feature is the oak ceiling installed by Gavin Dunbar about 1530, a truly medieval conception, not only architecturally but in the spirit in which it is decorated. Its 48 shields of arms, gaily painted and gilded, declare the universality of Christendom by displaying the blazons of its princes, among them Pope Leo X and the Holy Roman Emperor, Charles V. It is surely unique that in this building a Presbyterian congregation has worshipped for centuries under the arms of a Pope! Yet this too is characteristic of a city which has always been stubborn and slow in conforming to new causes.

The setting of St. Machar's is very beautiful. Sheltered from the north by parkland trees which hide a loop of the River Don, it faces the Chanonry. As its name records, this was formerly the quarter of the canons of the cathedral. Secluded gardens behind high stone walls now surround the houses of some of the University's professors, the choicest academic residences in Scotland, and indeed the whole of this part of the town has the atmosphere of a precinct, which it has been for several centuries. The Chanonry passes into the High Street of Old Aberdeen, and facing this is King's College. King's, founded in 1494 by Bishop Elphinstone, is built in the form of a quadrangle. Two sides of this are original. One of them incorporates the chapel which, like the chapel of the namesake college at Cambridge, is the chief glory of the place. There is none of Cambridge's soaring gothic splendour here, but none of the college chapels of similar size either at Cambridge or at Oxford can better it. Indeed, its three-sided apse cannot be paralleled at the two English universities. Pleasing as the exterior is,

the interior is even more interesting, because the professors and students of the University told the Reformers of the sixteenth century that their chapel was their own affair, with the result that its medieval state has been preserved with the minimum of interference. There is little enough medieval woodcarving surviving in Scotland and King's College Chapel has a high proportion of the total. In the choir are the original superb canopied oak stalls, with pinnacles and lacy tracery and relief work incorporating thistles and the grape-design which is a typical motif of Scottish wood-carving. All this is of date about 1500. The apsidal pulpit is a little later, and was given by Bishop Stewart to the cathedral, from which it was removed.

Old Aberdeen is bounded on the north by the Don. The original route northwards out of the town crosses the river by the Auld Brig o' Balgownie, a lovely single-arch bridge with a span of 20 yards, below which the salmon pools are black and swirling. Tradition has connected it with Robert the Bruce, but it seems in fact to have been built by Bishop Cheyn, who accepted the overlordship of Edward I and fled when the Bruce rose to power. It is a somewhat impressive structure, with an eerie legend attached to it that one day it will collapse under the weight of "a wife's ae son, and a mear's ae foal", a legend which used to fascinate Byron as a child and draw him—himself an only son— to lean over the parapet and look into the inky water. So much did the legend haunt him that he came to use it in the Tenth Canto of *Don Juan*. His obsession with being an only son no doubt fixed the legend in his thoughts. Curiously, the great five-arch granite bridge built further down the river about 1830, known as the Bridge of Don, was paid for out of the profits of a small property with which Sir Alexander Hay endowed the Auld Brig o' Balgownie in 1605.

Bounded by two rivers as she is, it is not surprising that Aberdeen is well provided with bridges, and the old Brig o' Dee, to the south of the city, is in some ways as interesting as the Brig o' Balgownie. It is a much larger affair, with seven ribbed arches, and was built about 1520 by bishops Elphinstone and Dunbar. Much of it was reconstructed at the beginning of the eighteenth century, and when, in 1842, the bridge was widened, great care was taken to replace the west face and so to maintain the medieval character.

Aberdeen perhaps came as near as any town in Britain to being the independent medieval city-state, although of course not on the extreme Italian model. Geographically, she was far enough away from the centre of government, whether in Perth, Stirling or Edinburgh, to make intervention difficult. She was therefore in the fifteenth century, it has been said, the most perfect example of an organised Scottish Royal burgh. The power of her town council was supreme. This meant rule through an oligarchy of leading guild burgesses, a somewhat aristocratic body partly recruited from the gentry of the surrounding country. Also freemen of the city, in a more limited way, but jealous of the town council's powers as in other Scottish burghs, including Edinburgh, were the burgesses of trade, the craftsmen and merchants. They were at the real core of independence. The crafts were well organised, and they contributed largely to the pattern of life in the city, with their pageants and feasts, culminating in the procession to St. Nicholas' kirk at Candlemas, with an abbot and a prior at its head dubbed the Lords of Bon-Accord. The present East and West churches of St. Nicholas are replacements of the ancient church. Unhappily the work of those medieval craftsmen of the city has largely disappeared: indeed all the medieval heritage of the city has gone, with the exception of the fabric and some of the furniture of the ancient churches. One might have hoped that the die-hard attitude of the citizens would have preserved more. In the burgh records under the date 16th June, 1559, the chaplains of St. Nicholas' Church urged the provost and town council to safeguard the "chalices, siluer wark, kaippis (cups) and ornaments" since it was learned that "certane personis in the southt partis of Scotland hes interpryssit at thair awin hands . . . to distroy kirks . . . and the ornaments and polacie of the same." Here we have the traditional Aberdonian suspicion of ongoings in other parts. But we find that two years later the precious things had been saved only for disposal to the highest bidder, the money to be "applyit for the commond weill." Where the treasures went we do not know.

There are, however, collections of distinction in the museums of the city. One of these is housed in the residence of a one-time provost, Sir George Skene of Rubislaw, an interesting building close to Marischal College. It is one of the very few vernacular buildings outside the Old Town, and was built about the middle of the sixteenth century and modified by Provost Skene rather more than 100 years later. It still possesses some of the original ceilings and mural paintings, and has been turned into a museum of old town life. Skene was one of the numerous body of Aberdonians who, over the centuries, forged a trading link with the Baltic and the Low Countries and through it influenced the way of life of their part of the country. Skene was a very successful Danzig merchant; but men from Aberdeen and the country near founded families in, for example, Sweden. The Swedish House of Nobles has had repeated injections of Aberdeen blood, and their arms are among the many Scots blazons displayed on the walls of that august chamber. The principal art collection in the city is in the Art Gallery, which also incorporates a regional museum. It is specially noteworthy for its modern paintings, Impressionist and later, which includes an extraordinary series of about a hundred portraits, mostly self-portraits, of contemporary British painters. The anthropological museum in Marischal College is too easily overlooked by visitors to the city. It interprets the subject liberally, and there is a great deal there which throws light on Scottish life and history, of the north especially, including finds of Viking and other material. Outstanding among its exhibits—although whether it will remain here permanently is in question—is the St. Ninian's Isle Treasure from Shetland, one of the most important finds of Viking silverware in Scotland, secured during a "dig" by a party from the University of Aberdeen. There is a fourth museum which I am tempted to mention, even if it is not open to public inspection and is in fact not really a museum at all. It is the house on the outskirts of the city restored and furnished by Mr. W. S. Bell. It is a seventeenth-century house, and its rooms are decorated and furnished with objects of art of this and the following century. I mention this house not with a view to stimulating the curiosity of visitors but because there are scores of such houses which could enrich the Scottish heritage if they could find owners of enterprise and good taste willing and able to reconstitute them in a similar way. There can be few countries which show less practical interest in their old buildings than Scotland does.

From many aspects the city seems dominated by Marischal College. The most modern part of the building (1906) fronts an inner quadrangle and is an essay in Perpendicular interpreted through the medium of local granite. Anachronistic though it may be, the impression it produces is a rather splendid one, and the myriad of sharp, clean white pinnacles against the skyline seen from a little distance compares well with the distant prospects of Cambridge or Oxford. There is something peculiarly appropriate in this hard, bright version of the Gothic. There could be no better symbol of the Aberdonian intellect, with its odd blend of philosophical inquiry with practical good sense. Dr. Alexander John Forsyth, the minister of Belhelvie, who in the early nineteenth century invented the percussion cap for guns, is an excellent example. But perhaps the man who illustrates it best, in himself and his descendants, is the seventeenth-century citizen David Anderson, known from his ingenuity as "Davie Do-a'-Things". He was a mechanic and his virtues were practical; but his daughter Janet, wife of the parson of Drumoak, was the mother of James Gregory, Professor of Mathematics in St. Andrews and Edinburgh and inventor of the reflecting telescope, grandmother of a Savilian Professor of Astronomy at Oxford and of another Professor of Mathematics at Edinburgh, and ancestor of Dr. Thomas Reid, the great opponent in Scotland of the scepticism of David Hume. Reid himself was a graduate and librarian of Marischal College.

The course of the Don is much less spectacular than the Dee, even in the higher reaches. The Dee's bed is granity, the Don's loamy. But the Don valley has been congenial to man for a much longer time, and the fields and villages feel ripe and lived-in. If appearances are not enough, one sure piece of evidence is to be found in the endowment of the churches in the larger villages. Several of these are in possession of fine silver Communion cups dating from the seventeenth century, and it is interesting that most of the Donside cups are in a style found almost exclusively in the north-east of Scotland. It is beaker-shaped, and it is one of the things which commemorate Aberdeenshire's link with the Continent, especially the Low Countries. King's College in Aberdeen and also St. Machar's possess very beautiful foreign cups in this style, finely engraved, presented by foreign students before the middle of the seventeenth century, and the parish church in the village of Ellon is the fortunate owner of a pair of beaker cups one of which carries the Amsterdam hall-mark and the other the punch of Walter Melvil, a silversmith of Aberdeen. Fintry, on the Don, has a pair of cups closely resembling the Ellon cups and obviously copied from them. Monymusk, a secluded village beside the river just where it begins to wind into the Grampian foothills, has no fewer than four such cups. They carry the date 1691, and the initials of the minister of that day, John Burnett, and the kirk session records have an entry under the date 18th January:

> The s^d day the Min^r represented to the Session how necessar it was to have four silver cups made for serving the Communion tables, and craved the mind of the Session anent it. Whereupon the Elders consented and ordered the Clerk to draw a commission to the young Laird of Monymusk to agree w^t some silver smith to make them at as easy a rate as he could.

Five months later it is recorded that the sum of £125 2s. has been disbursed for the cups. The name of the silversmith is not in the records, but his punch on the cups shows him to have been George Walker of Aberdeen.

Monymusk is associated with what is in some respects the most notable of Scotland's national relics: the Brecbennoch of St. Columba, otherwise known as the Monymusk Reliquary. This precious little bronze-and-silver mounted box is now preserved in the National Museum of Antiquities. It is supposed to have held the Psalter of Columba. Undoubtedly it was regarded as a sort of palladium of the Scots, for it was called the Cathach, or Battler, and Adamnan records that if it is sent thrice sunways round the army of Columba's clan, the Cinel Conall Gulban, they will return from battle victorious. The reliquary can be dated to the seventh or eighth century, and may well have been associated with the movement of Columba's relics from Iona to Dunkeld; but the first certain knowledge of it is its deposition in Arbroath Abbey at the beginning of the thirteenth century. It seems the Abbot of Arbroath invoked its powers by carrying it at the battle of Bannockburn. In 1415 it came to Monymusk and apart from a period with the Irvines of Drum it remained there until 1923, when the National Museum bought it from the Grants of Monymusk. It is a characteristic shrine of the old Celtic Church. Monymusk and the district around was a stronghold of this Church from the earliest times. If one goes due north from Monymusk to the village of Chapel of Garioch, there is an exceptionally fine carved monument called the

Maiden Stone, obviously associated with the rites of the primitive Church. There is a typical Celtic cross on one side, and the strange symbols of "centaur", "mirror" and "comb" all seem to be associated with the earliest Christians in the north, although they have never been interpreted. As might be expected, superstition and legend have accumulated round this stone, but the story which gives the stone its name has as its central figure a young beauty known as the Maiden of Drumdurno. She was baking cakes before her wedding, to take place on the following day, when a handsome stranger wagered her he could lay a stone "causey" right up to the Mither Tap of Bennachie before she had finished her baking, her heart to be the prize. She lightly agreed to what she thought a jest. The evening came down wet and dark when, looking out of the window for her true lover, to her horror she saw a great cloud on the top of Bennachie and a causeway complete up to the Mither Tap. She saw too the stranger coming for her and she recognised him for what he was, the Evil One. Flying desperately to Pittodrie Woods, she called upon heavenly powers and was turned into what is now called the Maiden Stone! There is in fact the remains of a stone causeway leading up to the Mither Tap, of uncertain antiquity, as there is evidence of the existence of an early fort on the Tap itself.

For a hill less than 1,700 feet in height, Bennachie has attracted surprising fame, both in legend and in verse. There is a stock of local ballads which sing of it and its guardian giant, Jock o' Bennachie, and, by contrary, of the Wee, Wee Man o' Bennachie. The most widely known of these ballads exists in versions which have been altered over the centuries and records the beauties of what is actually a modest and unassuming burn, the Gadie, in the parish of Garioch:

> *O! gin I war whaur Gadie rins*
> *At the back o' Bennachie.*

The sterner ballads, however, tell of an event which had its importance for all Scotland: the battle of Harlaw, in 1411.

> *Frae Dunideir as I cam' throuch.*
> *Doun by the hill of Banochie*
> *Allangst the lands of Garioch*
> *Grit pitie was to heir and se*

The noys and dulesum hermonie,
   That evir that dreiry day dud daw,
Cryand the corynoch an hie,
   "Alas, alas, for the Harlaw."

Harlaw was one of the three or four great critical battles in Scottish history, for it virtually decided whether Celt or Saxon was to shape the course of the country's future. It took place a mile or so north of Inverurie. Of all elements most troublesome to the Crown, Donald, Lord of the Isles, had invaded the north from his island stronghold and was sweeping all before him and threatening the destruction of Aberdeen. He had a force of probably 10,000 men, and he seemed to have it well within his power to break the grip of the Regent Albany on the country—the King, James I, being in captivity in England. The only hope lay in the Regent's nephew, the Earl of Mar. Mar was well known even in England and Flanders as a doughty knight, but on this occasion his knightly accomplishments were perhaps second to the ferocious spirit which he had inherited from his father, the notorious Wolf of Badenoch. He gathered such men as he could, but they are said to have totalled only about 1,000. They made up for their meagre numbers in discipline and determination. The Highlanders' attack was devastating, but Mar knew their methods and stood his ground. The battle was one of the bloodiest ever fought in Scotland and went on throughout the whole of that day, 24th July. Mar's losses were terrible. They included Sir Alexander Irvine of Drum, Leslie of Balquhan and his six sons, whose castle overlooked the battle, and the Provost of Aberdeen. But the losses of Donald were even more terrible, and when night fell he withdrew from the field. Mar was too greatly weakened to follow, but Albany himself pursued the advantage and forced Donald to make submission. Scotland breathed again, but as far south as the Lothians, as John Major records, boys played at Harlaw in their games.

North of Aberdeen the land juts like a bent knee into the North Sea. The district of Buchan, contained within the "joint" of the knee, has a famous name, but perhaps no part of Scotland is so little known to strangers. It is forbidding at first sight. The granite tableland is low, and although there is good farming there are big areas which seem bleak and inhospitable, for example in the district west of Peterhead. It has been called "a treeless land where beeves are good". In fact, it is a region of extraordinary interest, as full of character as the "broad Buchan" speech which is so hard for the outsider to interpret.

At the heart of Buchan is the village of Deer, now called Old Deer to distinguish it from a new village some miles to the west. There is nothing bleak about Old Deer. It is on the Ugie Water, well wooded, and pleasantly laid out around a late eighteenth-century church. The roots of the place, however, are in the ruined Abbey of St. Mary near by. It was founded by William Comyn, who acquired the earldom of Buchan by marriage, early in the thirteenth century. Or perhaps one should say they are in something much older than the abbey, the celebrated MS. known as The Book of Deer, which is preserved in the University Library at Cambridge. This MS. is all that is left of the seventh-century monastery founded by St. Drostan, one of the earliest strongholds of Christianity in the north, and in a sense it helps to embrace Buchan in the bounds of the Highlands, because it is the oldest surviving document written in Scots Gaelic, dating from the ninth century. Part of it is in Latin, and there are entries and marginal notes made in the first half of the twelfth century among which is the celebrated claim that the monastery was founded by Columba himself; but this is deliberate invention of a familiar kind, for much that has gone down to the credit of Columba should really be given to other early missionaries. Who St. Drostan was is a mystery, but it may be there was a Christian mission centred upon Deer even earlier.

Deer and its neighbour parishes in later times were the core of that Episcopalian resistance to Presbyterianism which I have mentioned in passing earlier in this chapter. William Meston, Professor of Philosophy in Marischal College, put their attitude into neat verse two centuries ago :

> They fear the Lord and till the ground,
> And love a creed that's short and sound :
> 'Tis true their speech is not so pointed,
> Nor with screw'd looks their face disjointed ;
> If scant of Theory, their Practice
> Supplies that want, which most exact is.
> They are not fond of innovations,
> Nor covet much new reformations ;
> They are not for new paths, but rather
> Each one jogs after his old father.

Meston was writing only half a century after the notorious "Rabble of Deer". This incident took place in 1711, long after the rest of Scotland was officially Presbyterian. An Episcopalian minister had been allowed by the Presbytery to retain the living of Old Deer, but now, six months after his death, a Presbyterian incumbent of the name of Gordon was presented only to find the church doors locked against him. The Presbytery called in help from Aberdeen, "to the number of seventy horse, or thereby", and a fight ensued in which the supporters of the Presbytery's nominee were "soundly beat off by the people, not without blood on both sides". It was claimed at the time that the Rabble of Deer procured the Acts of Toleration and Patronages. With Episcopalianism, of course, went strong sympathy for the Stewart cause, and the rabble are said to have seized the meat and wine prepared for the entertainment of the Rev. Mr. Gordon and to have drunk the health of the Pretender in the streets. This supplies some background for the Old Pretender's choice of nearby Peterhead as his port of arrival in 1715, on which occasion an Episcopalian clergyman prayed for his success in the Church of Deer.

The bounds of Buchan could be made an interesting, if exacting, circuit from Aberdeen for a long day around midsummer. For ten miles or more going northwards, the coast is rather featureless, although pleasant enough in fine weather. Then comes a deep, winding estuary at Newburgh, on the other side of which are the Sands of Forvie, which have recently proved of some interest for archaeological excavation. This is one of the largest areas of blown sand in Scotland, the weathered fringe of the great tableland. A little further north the rock outcrops have proved enduring, and on a headland beyond Cruden Bay the Castle of Slains is—to quote Dr. Johnson's *Scottish Tour*—"only a continuation of a perpendicular rock". This is an immensely impressive piece of coast, with veins of softer rock which the sea's action has worn away to form chasms and caves in variety. One cavern near Slains known as Hell's Lum is about 200 feet deep, with branching tunnels into which storms force the sea with awesome effect; but the most tremendous of these holes is the famous Bullers of Buchan, where on occasion the sea thunders through into a cauldron known as the Pot of Birss Buchan, the sandstone walls of which are something like 100 feet in height.

With Peterhead begins a chain of coastal towns and villages which are the bases of some of the toughest fishermen in the kingdom. Peterhead, the most easterly port in Scotland, is the natural refuge for storm-driven ships over a vast area of sea, and an Act of the Privy Council of Scotland in 1705 authorised a contribution for keeping the harbour in repair to be levied as far away as the three Lothians. Conditions have bred a stern race of men. Perhaps the most renowned of them is commemorated by a bronze statue beside the Town House. He is Field-Marshal Keith. Keith, like so many men of Buchan, took part in the 'Fifteen and was exiled for it, but he became an esteemed general in the Russian Army and finally a marshal of Frederick II of Prussia who, when he fell at the battle of Hochkirchen, buried him with honours in the garrison church of Berlin. Fraserburgh, just above the "knee" of Buchan, is another great fishing port. It was founded by Sir Alexander Fraser in the sixteenth century. In view of the current pressure for a fifth Scottish university, it is worth recording that Sir Alexander was granted the privilege of founding a university at Fraserburgh, with power to him and his heirs to appoint staff and determine the rules. This was confirmed by Act of Parliament in 1597; but what happened to the institution is lost in obscurity, except that half a century later the college buildings were requisitioned for students of King's College when the plague broke out in Aberdeen. Westwards from Fraserburgh are the picturesquely situated fishing villages of Rosehearty, Gardenstown and Macduff.

From Macduff southwards the Deveron forms a boundary of Buchan. The course of the Deveron here is very beautiful and comes to a climax at Bridge of Alvah near Montcoffer House, for the bridge spans the water between hanging woods at a height of nearly 50 feet. Where the Deveron turns westwards is the town of Turriff, built of the red sandstone on which it stands. It has a long history—indeed, it is referred to in The Book of Deer—but little that is old is left except for certain portions of the church, once quite rich in sixteenth-century frescoes.

It is a slight stretching of the bounds of Buchan to take the south-west exit-road from Turriff and follow it as far as Forgue. As if to flout the hard-bitten Episcopacy of Buchan, the kirk of Forgue happens to possess the oldest Communion cup used in the services of the Church of Scotland. It is an extremely beautiful cup of silver. The bowl of this cup carries the punch of Henry Thomsone, an Edinburgh silversmith, and also that of James Cok as deacon of the craft, a combination which indicates the date 1563. An inscription shows that the cup, with a companion piece, was presented to the church by James Crichton of Frendraught in 1633. Frendraught Castle, a mile or two to the south, was burned down in 1630, Viscount Melgum and the Laird of Rothiemay losing their lives. Frendraught was accused of murder and offered to stand trial, but an old servant was blamed and executed. Possibly the cups were a thank-offering for his escape.

One picks up the bounds of Buchan again at the Ythan river, which rises in Forgue parish in three springs called the Wells of Ythan. The Ythan is one of those Scottish rivers once famous for their pearl-fisheries, and tradition has it that a large pearl in the Crown of Scotland is an Ythan pearl. About a mile and a half south of the Wells, at Glenmailen, is an interesting site: the most northerly point known for certain to have been attained by the Roman legions. It is a marching-camp, a parallelogram in shape. Even to-day that high moorland offers a prospect only of rolling hills and far beyond that a grey waste of sea. One can imagine even Agricola's resolution weakening. The Ythan makes a great serpentine curve of many miles before winding into the policies of Fyvie Castle. Fyvie is one of Scotland's great houses. The original castle, in which Edward I stayed during his invasion progress through the north, is long since gone; and the present triple-towered pile is essentially a Renaissance building, a palace rather than a fortified place. The oldest part of it is the east tower, built in the fifteenth century by Sir Harry Preston when he was granted the lands of Fyvie on the battlefield of Otterburn. The Meldrum tower to the west is a sixteenth-century structure. Finally, Alexander Seton who, as Earl of Dunfermline, became Chancellor of Scotland, linked the two towers by building a central tower now given his name. He modified the existing buildings to make a symmetrical façade of the whole. The final touch is the enormous arched entrance which, true to the spirit of the style, bears no real relationship to the internal economy of the house. Odd as it is, this is a truly splendid residence, and it contains the finest circular stone staircase in Scotland, recalling similar features in the great *châteaux* of the Loire. We cannot leave Fyvie without mention of the stone trumpeter which tops a turret. It commemorates Andrew

Lammie, the Fyvie trumpeter and lover of Agnes Smith, the daughter of the miller of Tifty and heroine of the old ballad "Mill of Tifty's Annie". The miller and his wife opposed the girl's marrying a trumpeter, and so ill-used her that she died of a broken heart. Her tombstone—a restored one—on which she is recorded as dying in 1673, is in Fyvie kirkyard.

The stretch of the Ythan below Fyvie, like most of Buchan, is far from the tracks of tourists, but it is worth a deviation from the main route, for the wooded ravine the river has carved for itself is probably the loveliest piece of scenery in the north-east. The river skirts first the Braes of Fetterletter, then the Braes of Gight. The ruined remains of the castle of Gight command its Braes, but the castle's interest hangs mainly upon its associations. It was the home and stronghold of the Gordons of Gight for about 300 years, and left the family only in 1787, when Catharine Gordon saw it go to pay the debts of her husband, Captain the Hon. John Byron. On his mother's side, Lord Byron had an ancestry as stirring as any romantic poet could wish. Gight was the subject of several prophecies by Thomas the Rhymer, but they are feeble stuff beside some of the real chapters in the family history. There was, for example, the fifth laird, who for 30 years of the sixteenth century reigned as a tyrant over the district with the support of his seven sons; and in 1644 the castle was seized by the Covenanting army under Argyll, when the seventh laird escaped after being a prisoner. The most sensational of the Rhymer prophecies—

> *At Gight three men by sudden deaths shall dee,*
> *And after that the land shall lie in lee.*

—was not completely fulfilled until the nineteenth century, but this came as something of an anti-climax.

The Ythan continues its course through a beautiful countryside, by Methlick and Ellon, to the sea, so completing the bounds of Buchan. It is a countryside rich in the relics of human activity, from cairns on the hilltops and flint arrowheads—once known locally as elf-bolts—to medieval fortresses like Tolquhon and eighteenth-century mansions such as Haddo House and Victorian castles in the baronial style of Ellon. And when the defiant spirit of Jacobitism died, the men of Buchan turned their vigour into other fields, from the Peninsula to Fiji, and in the parish churches the tide of Empire has left innumerable memorials.

CHAPTER SEVEN

Elgin and
the Laigh o' Moray

Elgin is a town of wide horizons. If one comes to it from the high hills by way of Craigellachie, the sudden expanse of sky and horizon is breath-taking, under certain conditions almost oppressive. At first sight the surrounding countryside looks monotonous after the grandeur of the Cairngorms or the woods and hills of Strathbogie and Strathisla, and the town shows little of itself; but as soon as one penetrates the outer fringe of housing and comes into the cobbled streets with their stone walls and glimpses of gardens, the charm of the place begins to take effect; and by the time the sun has gone down beyond the Moray Firth and the pigeons disturbed by the chimes have fluttered down for the last time to seek their roosts, Elgin has made a place for itself among the memories of another stranger.

Elgin, like Edinburgh, is a town of two periods. There are not two distinct towns, as in the case of Edinburgh, for the periods mingle: vernacular, mainly of the seventeenth century, with Georgian work of the eighteenth and nineteenth centuries. The stone is the same light-coloured, locally-quarried freestone, whatever the period, and the result is a marriage of periods which has a peculiar charm of its own. The layout of the town is very simple: a long, gently curving street, the High Street, roughly linking the hill where the old castle stood with the cathedral on the low-lying meadows by the bank of the River Lossie. The High Street has its modern shop-fronts, but quite a number of fragments of the original street frontages survive. Dr. Samuel Johnson, in 1773, still found it possible to walk "for a considerable length under a cloister, or portico", and he remarks that this arcaded walk was probably continuous at one time, but that new buildings have intruded upon it. One of the best arcaded houses left is Braco's Banking House, at No. 7 High Street. The arcades have been filled in with shop-windows, but the form of the house is unspoilt, and there is a characteristic courtyard with white-washed houses behind. The date on one of the dormer pediments is 1694, and it was just after this that the banker, William Duff of Dipple and Braco, came to it. The house of Dean of Guild Ogilvie at 50 High Street is another good example of Elgin burgh architecture of the end of the seventeenth century. The wynds and closes which break the street frontage, if they have not the grandeur of the Edinburgh closes, are in some cases just as picturesque. The close behind the Ogilvie house recalls the Bakehouse Close in the Canongate of Edinburgh. Elgin too had its town mansions. The finest of them was Thunderton House, just off the High Street. Pieces of it have been scattered far and wide, and the plea for its restoration made by Mr. Ronald Cant in the Old Elgin Society's publication, now unhappily out of print, must be warmly endorsed. Charles Edward stayed at Thunderton House before the battle of Culloden, and Mrs. Anderson, his hostess, kept the sheets in which he slept and 25 years afterwards was buried in them.

The glory of Elgin, naturally, is the cathedral. The third largest in Scotland, it was called by Professor Hannah "the most satisfactory church that ever rose on Scottish soil". Elgin became the seat of the bishops of Moray in 1224, and the cathedral was completed before the end of that century. It was an enlargement of the existing Kirk of the Holy Trinity, and the building of such an elaborate structure so far north seems to have been due to the enthusiasm of Bishop Andrew de Moray, who at one time had been at Lincoln, and the munificent patronage of the king, Alexander II, and probably also to the support of the wealthy Norman lords who had been brought in to replace the rebellious element in Moray under Malcolm IV. The result was a lovely building which, although small in scale by English, to say nothing of Continental standards, was nevertheless choice of its kind and worthy of the title which it won, the Lantern of Moray. Only about a century after its completion it was partially destroyed by fire by the Wolf of Badenoch in revenge for a rebuke from the Bishop over the ill-treatment of his wife. The Bishop was broken-hearted over his church, famous as he said for its lofty belfries, its wealth of decoration and its jewels and relics, but slowly, over the next 100 years, it was restored. In 1402 it was threatened again, by Alexander, Lord of the Isles; but, in the face of a warning of excommunication, Alexander held his hand and part of his penance is said to have been the erection of the Little Cross at the junction of North College Street and the High Street, although it should be added that only the copestone of the existing

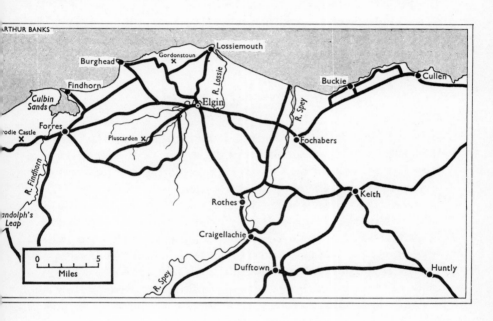

cross could conceivably be original. At the time of the Reformation, the cathedral was again a noble building, with twin-towered west front and lofty central tower, the whole surrounded by the group of manses known as the College of Chanonrie which still survives in the building now known, wrongly, as the Bishop's Palace, and the Deanery, now called the College. The Reformers did not destroy the cathedral directly, but the neglect which followed 1560 was just as sure in its effect. In 1567 the Privy Council ordered the stripping of the lead from the roof to be sold for money to pay the soldiers, although the cargo was lost at sea on its way to the Low Countries. There is probably some case for the disbelief of Dr. Johnson, who felt the order was intended primarily as a popular one. The weather, of course, did the rest. In 1640 the choir rafters were blown down; in 1711 the great central tower collapsed, demolishing the north transept in its fall; and from then on the ruins became a quarry and a refuse dump. At last, in 1809, steps were taken to remedy the situation. In due course a custodian was appointed, a poor, ne'er-do-well shoemaker called John Shanks. To his everlasting credit, his responsibility reformed him and he set about the clearing of the site with his own hands, moving 3,000 barrow-loads of rubble and collecting the fragments of stone-carving and laying bare the ground plan, so that the tablet to his memory bears an epitaph by Lord Cockburn:

> *Whoso reverences the Cathedral will*
> *respect the memory of this man.*

Now the ruins and the precincts of the cathedral have had some of their dignity restored so that even the empty shell, seen across the tree-studded lawns of the Cooper Park, is worthy of a cathedral city.

There is a curious link between the cathedral and Georgian Elgin. In 1748 a half-crazy woman called Marjory Anderson, widow of a soldier, made her home in the vestibule between the choir and the chapter house. She made a bed for her small son in the piscina and lived on such alms as she could get. Her son grew up, became a soldier like his dead father and went with the army to India. He rose from the ranks to become a major-general and built up a fortune of £70,000, which he bequeathed to found "the Elgin Institution for the Support of Old Age and the Education of Youth", otherwise known as the Anderson Institution. This handsome domed building lies at the east end of the town. At the further end of the town is an even handsomer Georgian building surmounted by a dome, Gray's Hospital, built in 1815. Set on a commanding site, it more than any other feature lends the town distinction in distant views over the wooded Morayshire plain. About midway between those two buildings, and at a point where the High Street widens to about 50 yards, is a third late-Georgian structure of distinction: the kirk of St. Giles. St. Giles is the town's patron saint, and the old Muckle Kirk dated from the twelfth century, so that it is regrettable that the original church was pulled down and replaced in 1826, but the Georgian building is very much a central feature of Elgin and one can scarcely think of the town without thinking of the pigeons wheeling around its belfry. This church possesses a pair of the beaker-shaped silver Communion cups mentioned in the last chapter as typical of the north-eastern counties. They were the gift of a provost, William Cummen of Achray, in 1681. The Rev. Thomas Burns attributed them to William Scott, the Elgin silversmith. Scott was not admitted a freeman of the burgh until 1701, but he was certainly working in the area. Several silversmiths worked in Elgin during the eighteenth century, so that the town must have been rather less primitive in its way of life than the late Dr. James Ritchie's essay on old-time Elgin suggests.

Many relics of old-time Elgin are preserved in the museum, which is close to the Braco house. The entrance hall in particular is rewarding, and it contains more than one example of the remarkable school of stone-carvers who seem to have worked at Burghead in Pictish times. The Picts were skilled drawers of animals, but there is nothing in their art quite as remarkable as the bulls of Burghead. With the greatest economy of line, these draughtsmen achieved a mixture of realism, symbolism and decoration. Or was there only one man who carved all the bulls? There were said to have been about 30 of the bulls at one time. What is probably the finest now graces the Edward VII Gallery in the British Museum, and two more can be seen in the National Museum of Antiquities in Edinburgh, leaving a mere couple of originals in the Elgin museum. It is a pity, I think, that the best showing of these things is not to be found here, in the locality where they were made and where the fertility rites with which they may have been connected took place, but Elgin's examples are fine works, nevertheless. Burghead itself may possess the bulk of them, unknown, for some may have gone into the packing of the south quay of the little fishing port.

The road to Burghead runs in long reaches northward out of Elgin through country at first sight bleak, but which, with its immense horizons, in the long run has a compelling attraction. The ground falls gradually towards a wide basin which is below sea-level, and which at no distant time was an arm of the sea. Later, the sea was cut off by the reef of sand and shingle which it threw up, and the basin became the

Loch of Spynie which, in the sixteenth century, was evidently a beautiful lake, fringed with rushes and trees. On an island in the midst of it stood Spynie Palace, residence of the Bishops of Moray, and this island is now a knoll with the ruins of the palace once magnificently furnished and surrounded by gardens and orchards. It was a stronghold as well as a palace, for with enemies such as the Wolf of Badenoch around the "Lords of Spynie" had to be prepared to use temporal might to defend themselves. How strong was their empire in every sense can be judged by Bishop David de Moravia's founding of the Scots College in Paris in 1313. The last of the bishops before the Reformation, on the other hand, had the reputation of keeping company with the Evil One, and if one walks down that lonely road in a summer gloaming it is not hard to call up the vision of the great flight of witches said to have been seen on All-Hallows Eve making for Spynie, and to imagine the weird light which glowed in welcome over the bishop's apartment.

A similar legend is associated with Gordonstoun, the entrance to which is at Duffus village, where the road breaks westwards to Burghead. Those all over the world who think of Gordonstoun as a famous but quite new public school are mostly unaware that its buildings have a long history. Gordonstoun House itself, now the central feature of the school, is a composite structure with early seventeenth-century wings, but the portion of the building between them has been remodelled in the eighteenth century. Seen from the great south lawn with its herbaceous borders, it is a gracious and rather lovely house. The original portions no doubt date from the day when the Marquis of Huntly was the owner, but long before then there was a fortified structure set in the midst of a bog for better defence. There are dungeons and secret passages in plenty in the present building which— the seventeenth-century pieces of it—passed into the possession of the Sir Robert Gordon who gave it its name. Those early Gordons had much need of dungeons and secret passages. They had the right of life or death—of "pit and gallows", in the old phrase—over their servants and tenants, and there was short shrift for any enemy who fell into their hands. Sir Robert, the first Baronet, was in good favour with James VI, and with Charles I too, which made it easier for him to plunder the countryside and to pursue his course of aggrandisement.

The most interesting of the Gordons, however, is brought to mind not by Gordonstoun House itself but by the odd building known as the Round Square. This was a series of stables and the like built on a circular plan, with a cobbled courtyard in the centre. The story goes that the Sir Robert who built it planned it circular so that the Devil could never get him into a corner, and there is no doubt that in his day this man had a sinister reputation, and was known as the Wizard of Gordonstoun. It was said that, when studying in Italy, he had made a pact with the Evil One, and that he had pawned his shadow to escape his clutches, so that even in the most brilliant sunlight he cast no shadow although his hat and his horse and all he carried retained theirs. He kept a furnace perpetually burning and in the heart of it brought to birth a salamander that would do whatever it was bidden. Finally, when the Devil came to claim his own, Sir Robert was reputed to have tricked him into giving him more time by declaring that the clock was fast, so that he might fly for sanctuary to the kirkyard of Birnie. The minister of Duffus fled with him, but fell behind, and when he was overtaken by a terrible man mounted on a black horse with two black hounds at its heels, the minister lied that he had not seen Sir Robert. But it was of no avail. Soon a distant yell of agony came to his ears, and the dreadful rider reappeared with the corpse of Sir Robert across his saddle-bow, the hounds still rending it. The minister of Duffus, for his attempt to save the laird, was found the following dawn dead with the marks of the hounds' teeth on his throat. Yet this same Sir Robert was, as one might have suspected, in reality, a man of learning, living where he was not appreciated, a man who shut himself away with his books because he had little in common with his neighbours. He invented, among other things, a sea-pump so efficient that it was used in the Navy, and this brought him into correspondence with Samuel Pepys, and another of his correspondents was Sir Robert Boyle, the great natural philosopher and enunciator of that Boyle's Law which every schoolboy knows. He must, therefore, look down with approval at the use which the school has made of his once notorious Round Square. The one-time stables have been turned into dormitories and common-rooms and what must be one of the most pleasing school libraries in the kingdom, and the cobbled courtyard has given way to a carpet of grass. One of the wisest parts of the policy of Dr. Kurt Hahn and his successors at Gordonstoun has been their determination to keep green the local traditions and to sink the school's roots deep in the soil of Moray.

If Gordonstoun has been restored to life by a change of use, Pluscarden Priory, some miles south of Elgin, has won back a new lease of its old life. It lies in a secluded, shallow valley through which the Lochty Burn flows, sheltered by woods and well placed to attract the maximum of sun: a good example of the skill with which the medieval monk selected the spot on which to build. It was, of course, a semi-ruin and roofless, and only in 1948 was it bestowed on the Benedictines of Prinknash Abbey in Gloucestershire, who sent some of their number to see what could be done. There are only a few of these men, but they have worked methodically and hard, consulting with an architect, and a great amount has been achieved. They have among them masons and a wood-carver and even an artist in stained glass, so that they are slowly bringing back some amenities to the abbey church, at the same time keeping themselves by cultivating the fields and building up a stock of bees. This is in accordance with the original rules laid down by the priory's mother church in Burgundy in the thirteenth century. In those days the stones were brought from nearby quarries by damming the burn and floating them down on rafts. While the brethren kept their vows of poverty and silence they exerted an excellent influence in what was a very turbulent district. They were respected locally, and won a certain reputation for scholarship through an account of Scotland's history called *The Red Book of Pluscarden*, written in the fifteenth century. Morayshire, however, is the Garden of Scotland: its fields are as fertile as its rivers are well stocked with trout and salmon. The labours of the monks of Pluscarden became the vehicle of temptation, for the priory grew rich and soon began to use its riches to acquire power. A Benedictine called John de Boys was sent from Dunfermline in 1470 to re-impose discipline for, as Professor Hannah puts it, "the light of their quire had not been reflected in the lives of the Valliscaulian monks".

The road leading west out of Elgin may have less obvious appeal than the roads winding south into the foothills of the Cairngorms, for after a mile or two it becomes a long, straight road with few features except occasionally a stand of pines. But in the distance appears a wooded hill with a monument atop of it, and this marks the town of Forres. It is an agreeable town with, oddly, one of the most beautiful cricket grounds in the kingdom, set in the shadow of the hill; but the most ancient and interesting object lies on the right of the road somewhere about the point where one crosses the town boundary if coming from Elgin. This is a stone monument 23 feet high called Sueno's Stone. It is prominent enough but, at present road-speeds, to miss it is possible. Sueno's Stone has proved baffling to archaeologists. The appearance on it of a cross inclines me to side with those who link it with the other Pictish stones associated with early Christianity in the north-east; but it is true enough that none of the other stones can show anything resembling the elaborate battle-scene of Sueno's Stone, with its chained captives and decapitated bodies. It is scarcely surprising that many efforts have been made to establish it as a memorial to a great victory: captives and corpses are usual enough as expressions of a mighty king's prowess in ancient Egyptian or Assyrian art. The most picturesque, and perhaps also the most credible, of these associations revives the tale of the invasion of Moray by Sigurd the Powerful, Earl of Orkney, in A.D. 900, when he was resisted by Maelbrigd, mormaer of the province, a grim-looking warrior with a single protruding tooth. He challenged Sigurd to a fight with 40 picked horsemen on either side, but the treacherous Sigurd put two men on each horse. Battle was joined, and inevitably the Northmen slew the men of Moray, cutting off their heads and hanging them from their saddle-bows; but Sigurd, with the ghastly head of Maelbrigd at his horse's flank, scratched his leg on that protruding tooth and, within three days, he died. The headless bodies carved on Sueno's Stone have identified it, for some, as the monument on Sigurd's grave. The Sueno whose name is now given to the stone was the son of Harald, King of Denmark, whose men routed the Scots under Malcolm II at Forres in 1008.

A granite boulder near by, but on the other side of the road, recalls that evil repute for harbouring the black arts already met with at Spynie and Gordonstoun, but which lingered for a long time over all this countryside. Forres's association with witches was so widely known that Shakespeare built *Macbeth* around it, and Boswell recalls how Johnson insisted on getting out of his carriage on their way across the "blasted heath" and declaimed the appropriate lines. Obviously there is little purpose in trying to identify a heath in a tale which Shakespeare read about in Holinshed, who lifted it from Boece, who wrote his chronicle far from the heath anyway; but this wayside boulder brings a piece of grim realism into the welter of superstitious tales. The very King Duncan whom Shakespeare used as the first victim in his bloody account is said to have been smitten with a puzzling disease after staying in Forres castle, and three local witches were seized and condemned for sorcery. Their fate was not unlike the fate of Regulus. They were jammed in barrels with spikes inside and pushed off the top of Cluny Hill. Three great stones marked the places where the barrels stopped, but only one of them has survived. These unhappy witch-hunts persisted in the Laigh of Moray, the Morayshire plain, until as lately as the seventeenth century, and a number of poor women were strangled and burned there even in the reign of Charles II. It brings uncomfortably near the dark age represented in *Macbeth*. As one whose clan is descended from Macbeth's father, the first Mormaer of Moray, I might perhaps say "misrepresented", historically speaking, for Macbeth was something of an heroic figure, in spite of his slaying of Duncan, and there may be something symbolic in the denigrating by after generations of this last Highland king of all Scotland.

The very fertility of this Garden of Scotland has helped to bring it into the mid-stream of history, but it has been curiously subject to natural as well as human disturbances. The lower course of the Findhorn river as it winds down through the foothills is among wooded dells filled with birdsong, and it looks one of the most idyllic little streams that it is possible to find. But on the Relugas policies there is a rocky feature called Randolph's Leap, and on the path down to it, high above the river, is a stone which they tell you—to the disbelief of most strangers—marks the height of the flood of 1829. The Findhorn is typical of these short Highland rivers with an enormous catchment area. Sir Thomas Dick Lauder left an enthralling eye-witness account of the 1829 disaster, seen from Relugas itself, where he was tenant. He tells how a black cloud gathered, filling the sky with darkness and the countryside with a bronze twilight; how it broke away to the south on the Monadhliaths, where the Findhorn rises; how a tempest arose that tore the limbs from the trees; and how a wall of water came down the little valley of the Findhorn carrying rocks before it making a noise like thunder and the cannonade of battle combined. At Dulsie Bridge the

17 Winter in Lochaber, Inverness-shire

water was 40 feet above the river bed. At Relugas itself the gardener caught a salmon with his umbrella 50 feet above what should have been the river. A wooded hill 100 feet high is said to have been swept away. And when this mass of water emerged on to the lower ground, carrying the new three-arched Findhorn Bridge with it, the whole plain of Moray seemed to be submerged under the muddy, foaming flood, with the sails of fishing vessels from the coast moving over it in search of survivors.

The Findhorn has proved fickle and unpredictable below Forres as well as above. There can be few places in Britain where the landscape has altered so much in a short space of years as between Burghead Bay and Culbin: that is, the lands flanking Findhorn Bay. There have been two ports of Findhorn before the present one. There is no record of the first, but the second had a harbour of considerable status right down to the end of the seventeenth century. The Findhorn skippers, as the late Dr. Ritchie has recorded, plied not only to the Scots ports, but as far afield as Rotterdam and Bordeaux, and the surviving lading lists make good reading with their cargoes of indigo, cloves, nutmegs, rice, their figs and prunes, their white Rhenish wines and "Ffrench" wines, their puncheons of vinegar and their ginger. The Garden of Scotland kept its lairds in good circumstances, as it had once kept its religious houses. Findhorn too built its own barques and fishing vessels. It was the port of Forres, which levied dues on the goods which came in there. But across the bay was an enemy which it could no more fight than Pompeii could fight Vesuvius, for the dunes of Culbin kept up an insidious attack on the harbour, filling its bottom until big craft could no longer venture and choking the river until it changed its course. On 11th October, 1702, a high tide combined with the river to flood the land and cut off the port entirely. The people had anticipated this and had left their homes, and the immense tides soon broke up harbour and houses until not a trace of the old port remained.

Natural forces of a different kind were at work on the other side of Findhorn Bay, and they are still at work. The Culbin sandhills are one of the most remarkable sights in Scotland, and it is difficult to believe they cover what was once a granary of the north. Hugh Miller describes how he wandered here for hours in the barony of Culbin, seeing nothing but a few stunted bushes and some withered bent-grass where,

18 Broadford Bay, Skye

in the middle of the seventeenth century, "had been the richest fields in the rich province of Moray". Here again disaster was foreseen. The Laird of Brodie, whose interesting old castle between Nairn and Forres, hid in the pinewoods, is still the home of Brodie of Brodie, described in his diary how during a succession of stormy seasons the seas were eating into the land while the sand gathered in great, threatening dunes near Nairn. Then one day in the late summer of 1676 the reapers were ready to bring in a bumper harvest. When night fell a great gale from the north-west sprang up, bringing with it the dunes which had been accumulating, and when dawn came there were two feet of sand covering the barley fields. Year after year this terrible invasion went on. The tide of sand advanced upon woods and farms, and finally buried the manor of Culbin. As one might expect in Morayshire, a sinister legend grew up around the event. Dr. Ritchie describes graphically how the Laird is said to have been playing cards late on a stormy Saturday night unheeding of the warning that the Sabbath was at hand, saying he would play even if the devil were his partner. At that there was a shattering clap of thunder and the Devil himself appeared in the chimney-place. He sat down and played with fantastic skill, so that his host did not notice the sand which by daybreak had buried the mansion in a huge mound. Indeed, the Laird is supposed to sit there still intent on his marathon game, and when in later years a chimney was exposed by a gale a venturesome man who called down it was answered by a peal of such dreadful laughter that he fled. Well, it is true enough that gales have laid bare many ruined homes buried in the dunes, as well as coins and pottery, and the artifacts of much earlier times; but there can be no question of ever driving back the invading dunes to get at the rich fields beneath. What is in fact being done to-day is to arrest the advance of the dunes, first by planting grasses to bind them and control them, and then by planting conifers which are already covering considerable areas of the dunes with plantations. Much of the Culbin hills is now under an afforestation scheme, and the gigantic effort to check a natural disaster is in its way as spectacular as the sand invasion.

CHAPTER EIGHT

Inverness
and Inverness-shire

At this point in the book I am faced with a difficult choice. Up to this point, the plan has been to select a centre, of special interest in itself, and from which a selection of interesting, significant places could be reached with ease. But from now on we enter the essential Highlands, a region of mountain massifs and long sea-lochs, of vast tracts of almost untenanted country with a thin sprinkling of villages and only a handful of towns, none of them really very old. The choice lies between a succession of short chapters, each based on one of the little towns, or a pattern similar to the one I have followed, involving far longer excursions from a very few bases. I choose the second alternative. Communications in the furthest Highlands are so restricted that to base oneself at any point in their heart means, in most cases, that one can move only in two directions, backwards or forwards. To have freedom of movement in the Highlands, as General Wade found out long ago, one must withdraw to the roots of the big valley systems.

The hub of the Northern Highlands is Inverness. It is without rival, too, for the title of capital of the Highlands. Its commanding position can be sensed at once, and dramatically, by anyone coming to it along the long, straight road out of the Morayshire plain. The cloud-capped hills of Sutherland far across the Moray Firth swing nearer with every mile westwards until the mass of Ben Wyvis ahead begins to dominate, and then as range upon range materialises to west and south also, the spires and smoke of Inverness show in the midst of an amphitheatre of hills. Even beyond the town is a glint of the sea, the shallow fjord of the

Beauly Firth; and unseen on the other flank is the huge channel of Loch Ness and Loch Lochy, linking this east-facing town with the whole complex of the western seaboard and the isles. It is small wonder that so much history has been routed through this town, from the coming of Columban Christianity in the sixth century to the going of the divine right of kings after its final defeat in the eighteenth.

There is, however, little in the town to-day to remind us of this history. It is a town with many attractions, but not a great deal of distinction. By that I mean it is a pleasant place to put up in, especially if one finds lodging in the west part of the place, where there are handsome houses giving on to the Ness. There is something rather Continental about this part of the town, particularly in the half-light of a summer evening, for the shallow river is wide and impressive and curves gracefully and with a dignity out of all proportion to its five or six miles of length. The lights are gay, and the flower-beds glow gaily under them. At the same time, the winds that blow in from west or south are hill winds, untainted, and sometimes they seem to carry the faint tang of peat-smoke or even of bog-myrtle or the honey-smell of bees. But one looks in vain for the fragments of the past which one stumbles on in Elgin or in Aberdeen. The castle, for all its fine outline and vaguely fortified appearance, turns out on inspection to be the county offices, erected in 1835, and the Gothic towers across the river are found to be the episcopal cathedral of St. Andrew, built in 1866. It is a pity it is without an ancient precinct to help in recapturing its past. If we are to believe the egregious Mr. Burt, there was nothing worth preserving even in his day, the middle of the eighteenth century, for he has left a picture of squalor and ugliness and abject poverty; but Burt's journal of his travels in the north is notorious as probably the most bilious travelogue ever written, reaching its celebrated climax with his reference to the hideousness of the Highland hills, "especially when the heather is in bloom". His record is too jaundiced-sounding to be true, and the explanation has been put forward that, as he was "neither an officer nor a gentleman", he was denied entry to circles which would have satisfied even his fastidious taste. There is no doubt the Inverness of his time must have contained a very interesting and picturesque society, men and women in whom the pride and prejudice of their past seethed the more because their way of life was doomed. They were accustomed to live well, to dress splendidly, many of them were cultivated and had, for the Britain of their time, the extraordinary accomplishment of speaking English, Gaelic and French with equal ease; yet they still had a feudal outlook and could boast followers ready to shed blood as soon as hear their names belittled.

To illustrate how the Inverness of those days was a meeting-point of old and new, I cannot resist citing Macdonell of Glengarry. He was a chief who lived in the past. His portrait by Raeburn hangs in the

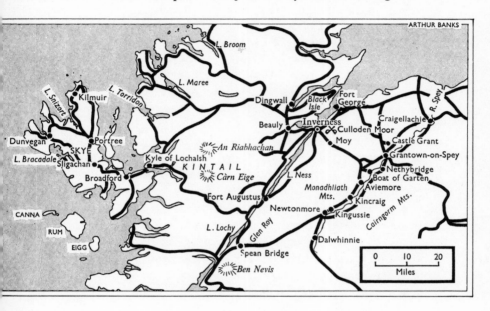

National Gallery of Scotland, and I can vouch for the extravagance of the weapons which he carries in the portrait, for they still exist in private possession, and I have had the pleasure of handling them. He was the original of Fergus MacIvor in *Waverley*. Scott knew him well and called him "a kind of Quixote in our age": indeed, Scott's faithful staghound was his gift. But when he travelled it was with his "arms and his tail"—his weapons and his armed retinue—and when he was authorised to raise a regiment, the Glengarry Fencibles, on his estates, he turned out of his property any man who disobeyed his order to join the regiment, because he had "refused to serve me". The most colourful

incident recorded about this survivor from feudal times began at a ball
given in Inverness on May-Day, 1798. A certain Lieutenant Macleod of
the 42nd had the temerity to secure a dance from the belle of the ball,
Miss Forbes of Culloden, in spite of objections from Glengarry.
Glengarry picked a quarrel and challenged Macleod, who died of the
wound he got in the duel. The Chief was indicted for murder and, on
the advice of his counsel, Henry Erskine, surrendered to the authorities
to stand his trial, which duly took place before the High Court of
Justiciary in Edinburgh. Glengarry was acquitted, but his counsel
refused to attend the dinner held to celebrate the verdict.

The duel took place not in Inverness itself, but near Fort George, at
the other end of the Inverness Firth. The fort is worth a visit. Not only
is it a symbol of the pacification of the Highlands after Culloden, the
process which made Glengarry an anachronism, but, as Mr. Stewart
Cruden says in *The Scottish Castle*, it is a text-book example of a
garrison fortress and unique as a professional job in mid-eighteenth-
century military architecture. It was too grimly efficient for its purpose
to have a stirring history. The original Fort George was built by Wade
in 1726, but when the Jacobite army occupied Inverness early in the
spring of 1746 the Highlanders seized the fort after a two-day siege and
blew it up. The new fort was designed about 1747 by William Skinner,
Director of Engineers, and occupies the point of a peninsula, its base
protected by a ditch crossed by a long bridge with drawbridges. There
is no better place to study the eighteenth-century idea of a defensive
work. "The most considerable fortress and best situated in Great
Britain", is the comment of James Wolfe, later the hero of Quebec,
who saw Fort George while it was building.

Wolfe, incidentally, has left some interesting comments on the
battle of Culloden, the field of which he revisited in 1751. The tale is
well known how Cumberland, smiled at contemptuously by a wounded
Highlander after the battle, turned to Wolfe and ordered him to shoot
the man. "My commission", Wolfe replied, "is at your Royal Highness's
disposal, but I can never consent to become an executioner." Wolfe's
afterthoughts, however, are less well known. He saw little glory in the
victory; but it is disturbing to find he thought the massacres a military
necessity and regarded the people of the Highlands as villains and
brutes.

The battlefield is only about five miles east of Inverness. There is little to see there, but a pilgrimage to it is recommended, if only because the few melancholy graves stir up thoughts about its significance. The fate of the Highlands was decided in 40 minutes, and in that brief span you have the Highland character in a nutshell. First came the spell of impetuous bravery, when the Mackintoshes anticipated orders and led the whole right of the Jacobite line against two-to-one odds and shattered the first rank of the Hanoverians, only to fall under the bullets of the second. Then, when an equally furious rush from the left might still have restored the situation, came the incredible sulk of the Macdonalds. Though the Duke of Perth exhorted Glengarry's regiment and said he would call himself a Macdonald for the rest of his life, though Keppoch threw himself on the enemy almost alone and died crying that the children of his tribe had forsaken him, the Macdonalds, simply because they had not been given their traditional place of honour on the right of the battle-line, marched coldly from the field! The impatience and petty pride of the Celt between them lost the day. The rest of the story, on the Highland side, is of heroic individual fights against hopeless odds: John Mor M'Gillvray who slew 12 men with his broadsword before the pikemen got him, the mighty Golice Macbane who, sorely wounded, set his back to a turf wall and accounted for 13 of a troop of dragoons before they cut him down.

Culloden may have little military significance, as Wolfe said, but even after two centuries it can stir Scottish feelings as neither Bannockburn nor Flodden can do. The main reason, undoubtedly, is the inhuman behaviour not only of Cumberland but of large numbers of his men in the weeks that followed the battle, and no number of attempts to whitewash the "Butcher" can dispose of the records of his own words, whether they be the contemptuous reference to Lord-President Forbes as "that old woman who talked to me of humanity" or his orders as to how the inhabitants of Inverness-shire should be treated. And endeavours to put the whole blame for the blackest page in British military history on the Hanoverians leave unaccounted-for the approval of such men as Wolfe. It is true that some of the severest critics of the butchery were English ones; but Scots almost to a man side with the Highlanders over Culloden because in its aftermath they sense what it feels like to be treated, on one's own soil, as a tribe beyond the pale. Of course those clansmen were wild, dirty, coarse-feeding, crude-living creatures, whose habits at the time of Culloden were as repugnant to any citizen of Edinburgh or Glasgow or Aberdeen as they were to any gentleman from the south; but we cannot forget that in the five months during which Charles Edward was a fugitive among the hills not one of the hundreds of savage tribesmen who knew his movements would have sullied his honour by betraying him for the price of £30,000 set on his head. The only man who entertained traitorous thoughts, Coll Macdonald of Barrisdale, was no poor clansman.

Inverness-shire is an enormous county, stretching from the spine of the Grampians out into the Hebrides. In this as in the subsequent chapters, historical or other objectives of the sort we have been dealing with may be buried in such spectacular scenery that they are overwhelmed by their settings. Speyside, for example, is full of things worth going a long way to see, but they are always dominated by the magnificence of the strath itself. This is apparent after a few miles down the Great North Road out of Inverness. After passing Moy Hall, seat of the Mackintosh of Mackintosh, chief of the great group of clans known as the Clan Chattan, and crossing the Slochd Mor summit, there opens what is probably the most wonderful panorama in Britain. On an early summer afternoon from here the Cairngorms achieve a grandeur greater than from any other point. Their true name of Monaruadh, the Red Mountains, is explained by those ruddy flanks contrasted with the purple-blue of cloud shadows and the lacings of snow in the northern corries. Strathspey lies in a sweep of fertile green meadows and dark woodlands at the foot of these mountains, sheltered on the west by the Grey Mountains, the Monadhliath.

Strathspey is the country of the Grants. For nearly six centuries the Clan Grant has dominated it, from the village of Craigellachie, where the Spey turns north into the plain of Moray, down to the craggy ridge of the same name near Aviemore which gave the clan its ringing battle-cry of "Stand Fast, Craigellachie!" surely the most rousing of all clan rallying-calls instinct with that strength-from-mother-earth quality round which the ancients wove the legend of Antaeus. Indeed, for me, between these two points the Spey, now swift and tawny, now slowing to an inky salmon-pool, is the choicest river in Scotland. The heart of

the Grant country is, of course, Grantown itself, a deliberate creation
of Sir Ludovic Grant and Grant of Grant, who invited merchants and
others to take feus in the year 1765. What until then had been moorland became the attractive town of to-day, with that wide square which
is typical of some of the best towns in the north. Sir Ludovic was one
of the eighteenth-century "improvers" of Scotland. His home was at
Castle Grant, a mile or two north of the town. Castle Grant, unhappily,
is now only a shadow of itself. Forty years ago it was still occupied, in
late summer at least, by American millionaires who rented its extensive
grouse-moors; but it suffered the fate of so many of these Highland
castles used by troops during the war, and the last time I saw it there
were broken windows and flapping blinds. Not that it was one of the
handsomer castles: Queen Victoria likened it to a factory. But it was
an historic house, filled with interesting relics. Some of them were
still there a few years ago. They included some at least of its unique
collection of Highland guns, a rare and beautiful type of firearm with a
Moorish look about it, the greater part of the two dozen surviving
examples of which were housed under this roof. One of these guns
appears in a portrait known as "The Champion" which hangs—or
hung?—on the walls of the castle. As lately as the beginning of the
nineteenth century great state was still maintained at Castle Grant,
and a contemporary description is interesting as showing what was
probably even then the usual practice in a chief's household. It is drawn
from that wonderful source-book, the *Memoirs of a Highland Lady*,
written by Mrs. Grant of Rothiemurchus.

> "Generally about 50 people sat down to dinner there in the great
> hall. . . . There was not exactly a 'below the salt' division so
> marked on the table, but the company at the lower end was of a
> very different description from those at the top, and treated
> accordingly with whisky-punch instead of wine. Sir James Grant
> was glad to see his table filled, and scrupulous to pay fit attention
> to every individual present; but, in spite of much cordiality, it
> was all somewhat in the king style, the chief condescending to the
> clan, above the best of whom he considered himself extremely."

The persisting feudalism of such a gathering underlines the heirarchy
of the clan system. It should also be noted that the traditional drink of a

gentleman in the Highlands was wine, the wine imported from Bordeaux in such quantities, not the crude spirit called whisky which the caterans brewed in their stills among the heather. Whisky, in the higher levels of Highland society, was probably regarded as a useful medicine for keeping out the cold, but by men of taste as fire-water fit for gillies.

Beyond Castle Grant the road winds up through fields and pine-plantations to emerge on the Dava Moor. On a glorious day this is one of the finest moorlands in the country, and it is a good plan to take the by-road which breaks west before the main route forks to Forres and Nairn and circle back by the B-class road across the moor. The by-road passes Lochindorb. On an island in the loch are the ruins of a castle, the traditional stronghold of the Wolf of Badenoch. This lonely castle had a colourful history behind it long before it came into the keeping of the Wolf in 1371. In the previous century the Comyns were lords of Badenoch. Its most famous occupant was Edward I, the Hammer of the Scots, who brought such a great army of knights, men-at-arms and bowmen down across the moors that the Comyns left it to retreat deeper into the hills. If one stands alone by the shore of Lochindorb, with no sound but the wail of a curlew, the determination of Edward which drove him to penetrate so far into a hostile region becomes clearer than any history book can make it. He is even said to have strengthened the defences of the castle in the 10 days he stayed there. Five centuries of neglect have reduced the castle more effectively than any siege could have done, but it is said to be possible to trace the water dungeon, a grisly prison under the level of the loch so that its floor was always under three feet of water.

Following the Spey southward past Nethybridge and Boat of Garten to Aviemore, the landscape changes constantly. The soil is much deeper than in the Western Highlands, and so the vegetation is richer. Natural history is not the concern of this book, but it is worth remembering that here, on the right bank of the Spey, in Rothie-murchus, are to be found remains of the ancient Caledonian Forest. This immense forest once covered a great part of the Highlands, and one of its glories was the old Scots Pine, with its red bark and its beautiful bottle-green foliage. There are still some trees surviving from the ancient forest in Rothiemurchus. Partly the destruction has been caused by climatic changes over two millennia; but for the past 1,000 years man has been mainly responsible for what has been lost. Lawless characters like the Wolf of Badenoch burned the woods about the ears of fugitives, and one of the means of hunting down both wolves and human marauders, as Dr. F. Fraser Darling has pointed out, was to burn down the forests. Jacobites no doubt were smoked out in the same way. Then came the iron-smelters. Indeed, from Elizabeth's day onwards they began looking in the Highlands for the timber for charcoal which they had been prohibited from taking in the south. And the two World Wars have completed the picture, what with the introduction of Canadian lumber-jacks who left graveyards of stumps sawn off several feet from the ground and fire-happy commandos encouraged to forget their inhibitions. Even so, there are some patches of beautiful forest land, with an under-cover of heather and blaeberries which fill the woods with heady, aromatic scents. The background of the mountains themselves is, at first sight, curiously tame seen from the river, except when near Aviemore the deep gash of the Lairig Ghru pass becomes visible, sometimes with dark clouds in its throat; but the rounded outlines of the Cairngorms are typical of granite hills, and one must go up into their fastnesses—the usual route is from Aviemore by way of Coylumbridge to Loch Morlich, or to the Lairig— to discover how scenically tremendous granite hills can be. There are no more spectacular places in the Highlands than the Garbh Corrie of Braeriach, or the Shelter Stone by Loch Avon—pronounced A'an—in the shadow of Cairngorm.

Kingussie is worth a visit, if only for the Highland Folk Museum now established there for a number of years. This museum was conceived and built up by Dr. I. F. Grant, distinguished for her books on Scottish social and economic history, and it is appropriate it should find a home in the Grant country, although she first brought her collection together on Iona and then transferred it to Laggan. It is now administered by a committee and is the responsibility of the four Scottish universities. Dr. Grant originally christened it Am Fasgadh, meaning The Shelter, but this name has been dropped. She saved from neglect and destruction numerous byegones and relics from remote homesteads and farms all over the Highlands, and the collection is now the most representative one ever likely to be, as the humble objects and materials which it contains are, many of them, of a sort which are thrown into ditch or rubbish dump. Here one can find varieties of the *cas-chrom*, the traditional hand-plough, of churns, of tinkers' tools; but there is also a great deal of more sophisticated material, including furniture, Highland costume and examples of the weapons carried by the clansmen.

Pointing south-west from Inverness is Glen Albyn, the Great Glen. It forms one of the most dramatic geological features in the country, and on the map it seems almost to sever the north-west Highlands from the rest of Scotland, which indeed it does with the help of the Caledonian Canal. The Great Glen is the result of two forces: a tremendous fracture of the rocks, followed by the flow of glaciers to south-west and north-east. In the fissure or fissures have collected the waters of three lochs, Ness, Oich and Lochy. Loch Ness, nearly 22 miles long, is the greatest volume of fresh water in the United Kingdom, and this it achieves mainly by its tremendous depth, 754 feet at the deepest point. The surrounding hills plunge steeply into it, and at one point at least there is more than 600 feet of water a little more than 100 yards from the shore. All this may help to give the loch its rather sinister reputation. The legend of a monster in its depths is a very old story, and the fact that the loch's bottom is about 700 feet below sea-level has led to speculations about the coming and going of some sea-creature by way of deep submarine fissures. All this is exciting, if unconvincing. The very fact that the loch is so deep brings in the awkward factor of pressures, and the steepness of the sides and poor aeration of the depths actually make for poverty of living forms. Nevertheless, hundreds of people claim to have seen something, and more than one serious naturalist has taken an interest in the problem. The ubiquitous Mr. Pennant in the eighteenth century does not seem to have anything to say on the subject, but he records an equally extraordinary phenomenon. On 1st November, 1755, when the great earthquake was destroying Lisbon, the waters of Loch Ness "rose and flowed up the lake from east to west with vast impetuosity . . . continuing ebbing and flowing for the space of an hour; but at eleven o'clock a wave greater than any of the rest came up the river, broke on the north side and overflowed the bank for the extent of 30 feet." Clearly this is no ordinary loch. But the vicinity of the Great Glen has many natural phenomena, and among the

19   Blaven in Spring, Skye

most celebrated of them are the Parallel Roads of Glen Gloy and Glen
Roy, near Spean Bridge. These gigantic terraces, several miles long and
at precisely the same levels on opposite sides of the glen, were once
reputed to be hunting roads of the heroes of Celtic legend, paths along
which the deer herds were driven for the convenience of Fingal and his
friends. The explanation, first hit upon by Agassiz about 1840, is that
they are beaches of a lake, at first deep, then receding, dammed in the
glens by a glacier perhaps 1,300 feet thick coming off what is now
Ben Nevis.

The Caledonian Canal, which links the lochs in the Great Glen and
makes it possible for sea-going vessels to pass from the west coast to the
Moray Firth, came about in a way that is little known. Emigration from
the Highlands had reached tremendous proportions by the year 1800,
entire clans sometimes following their chief to America. It was, of
course, an after-effect of the disruption of the Highland way of life by
the repressive measures which followed the 'Forty-five. The Government had become so concerned that it sent the celebrated engineer,
Thomas Telford, to investigate and report. He recognised the danger
of draining the Highlands of their best element. His remedy was to
open up the region to trade by building roads and by constructing a
canal through the Great Glen. The schemes went ahead almost at once.
They had an immediate effect in that they employed something like
6,000 men. In a few years coaches and post-chaises were running
where no such things had been seen, on country roads at least; and in
1822 the canal was opened with the passage of a steam-boat, after great
difficulties had been overcome. Telford engineered both roads and
canal, building the latter with its locks large enough to take the largest
British or American traders or, if necessary, a 32-gun frigate.

West of the Great Glen there are hundreds of square miles of roadless country. Here are some of the great deer forests of the Highlands:
Guisachan, Fasnakyle, Glencannich, Strathconon, Glencarron and many
more. Here too are such splendid mountain massifs as An Riabachan,
Carn Eige and Mam Soul, Ben Attow and the Five Sisters of Kintail.
The hydro-electric schemes have opened up the country considerably,
with well-engineered new roads leading up to the dams and power-
stations, but these cannot change the nature of the landscape. To our
eyes it is splendid, though desolate in some seasons; but when Dr.

Johnson journeyed by way of Glen Moriston and Glen Shiel he expressed himself as "astonished and repelled by this wide extent of hopeless sterility". It was this route, however, flanked by spectacular peaks and ultimately winding high above the north shore of Loch Duich, which impelled the Doctor to record his journey in print. The road next touches Loch Alsh and, after circling round among craggy hills, comes suddenly in view of the sea and of the Isle of Skye, with the bristling peaks of the Cuillin crowning it.

It is a measure of the size of Inverness-shire that here in this island of the Inner Hebrides one is still in the county administered from a town within scent of the North Sea. Even to-day the pace of life is different from the pace at the eastern end of the county. It resists the speeding-up process which the sophisticated world mistakes for progress. Even the fast car which eats up the miles down Loch Ness-side and on the hydro-electric roads has to slacken pace before it comes in sight of the sea-lochs, as the roads narrow and switch-back; and once over the ferry at Kyle of Lochalsh it can begin to seem a very long road indeed, with its detours and its passing-places and the sun so low and blinding in the west that one creeps into a golden haze in which dark crags and silvered arms of the sea loom and gleam fitfully. And it is not only the roads which slow life down, for in spite of increased mechanisation the land cannot be coaxed to increase its yield to satisfy any ordinary farmer. The soil is too thin, too sour, and in these high latitudes the growing season is too short. There is too an enervating quality in the air, for the heavy summer rainfall of these hill-girt coasts drenches the air and the drift from warmer seas takes much of the bite out of the wind even in winter. It is a country in which to work is to toil, in which the alternative to fierce effort is indolence and the alternative to fighting is dreaming. There is a passage in Alexander Smith's classic *A Summer in Skye* in which he describes the Fairy Room at Dunvegan, and the picture he draws of broadswords, dirks and mail rusting into a red ruin in the humid Atlantic airs, of the tattered flags that had once been darkened by the smoke of battle, of the faded papers spilling from a charter chest, all this in a half-twilight in which "the merriest sunbeam became grave", captures a mood into which it is easy to slip on the islands, however allergic one is to Ossianic fables. The only change in Dunvegan since Smith's day is that it now treasures its past history more carefully and methodically. The heir still must drain the silver-mounted horn of Rory Mor, the Fairy Flag has not yet been waved for that third and last time after which it will lose its power to succour the Macleod in his dire need.

In Skye, as in most of the western seaboard, man's works are so overshadowed by the scenery that the hard facts of history seem thin on the ground. It is true enough that much of the main stream of history passed this remote region by. In this respect, however, the scene is deceptive. There have been periods of great activity here, although most of it is unchronicled. The landscape is not as empty as it seems. At many points near inlets of the sea there are clutters of stones on knolls or crags which, on closer examination, show themselves to be walled structures now, in most cases, destroyed nearly to ground level. There are clusters of them by Loch Bracadale and at the head of Loch Snizort. They are remains of that structure unique to Scotland, the broch, which is scattered most thickly in the north and north-west, a circular stone fort with living quarters in the walls and a central courtyard, usually provided with a well. Their period is around two thousand years ago, although many of them were tenanted long after this. Local superstition ascribes them to the demons of the mist, a very convincing tale in the dusk when what has been called the grey wind is blowing in from the Minch; but their builders were an industrious, tough people, and the late Professor Gordon Childe believed them to be the castles of a conquering aristocracy, Mr. T. C. Lethbridge identifying them with the Picts. On the one hand, they imply dangerous times, for they are very strong defensive works. On the other hand they point to a well-organised and well-established community, and they are usually on or close to good land such as the *machair*, the grassy verge to the shore, which is limed and made fertile by the coral sand common in these parts. Mr. Lethbridge significantly reminds us of the immemorial sea trade-route which ran up the western coast of Britain from Cornwall to Cape Wrath. The broch-people could well have existed profitably on its fringes, plying between their settlements in fleets of coracles.

In later times, of course, this sea-route was utilised in reverse by the Northmen, who also left their settlements on its shores. They left numerous traces of Scandinavian culture in the form of jewellery, and some carvings such as the wonderful set of bone chessmen found in Lewis, some of which are in the National Museum of Antiquities in Edinburgh and the rest in the British Museum. The far origins of some of the trade going on at this time are underlined by coins found at the Storr Rock, some miles north of Portree. Some of the coins were Anglo-Saxon, some Oriental. In one sense, Skye in those far-off times was less remote from great centres of population than she became later. But indeed, right down to the disastrous aftermath of the 'Forty-five Skye had more trade-links with the Lowlands and with England than might be thought and many a field that has gone back to the heather fattened cattle for markets as far off as Yorkshire. The gravestone of Flora Macdonald at Kilmuir, looking across the Minch to the Hebrides, is a reminder not only of romance but of the fact that a Skye lady of two centuries ago had education and poise enough to win the admiration of such a cosmopolitan as Dr. Johnson.

CHAPTER NINE

Dornoch
and the Far North

The present chapter embraces all Scotland north of a line drawn west-wards from the Beauly Firth. It is not only an enormous area, but the roads are few and much of it is impenetrable except on foot. If we add to it, however sketchily, the Shetlands and Orkneys and the Hebrides, it becomes clear we must select a few significant things to speak for the whole region.

Dornoch is the centre I have chosen from which to scan this great region. It is not typical of the whole, but it is interesting in itself. It occurs about half-way up the intermittent belt of sandstone which hugs the coast between Beauly and the tip of Caithness, which means it lies in a landscape gentler than the hinterland of gneiss and schist and granite, the lonely moors and tarns which comprise so much of Sutherland and Wester Ross. Its roofs and towers and trees break the flat horizon of links and sea.

Dornoch is a tiny town to be a Royal burgh and the county town of Sutherland, but it lacks nothing in grace and dignity. Its spacious main square has that curious atmosphere, a mixture of a Continental air with austerity, which one meets with in some Scottish towns. The central feature is, of course, the cathedral which can be seen from miles away. The original church was built by Bishop Gilbert de Moravia, who took over the diocese in 1223, but this was burnt in 1570 in the course of a local feud. The building passed through various vicissitudes until, in the middle of the nineteenth century, it was the victim of one of those bad restorations of which the Victorians were capable, much of the original work being hidden. The tower is old, and so is the west window, and in general the exterior is pleasing. In the interior, the piers and arches which carry the tower are original, of the local sandstone, and so are the chancel walls, although they are weathered by the long period when the place was roofless. The most interesting feature in the nave is the effigy of Bishop Gilbert's brother, Sir Richard, who was killed by the Northmen at the battle of Embo. He is fully armed, a surcoat covering his hauberk, and his crossed legs seem to indicate he took part in a crusade. The effigy is sadly defaced; but, as Dr. Douglas Simpson has remarked, its defacements cannot obliterate its beauty. There is a good Chantrey statue of the first Duke of Sutherland near the west end, and Sutherlands have been patrons of the church for many centuries. Sixteen earls of Sutherland are believed to lie in the cathedral. The palace of the bishops, now an hotel, is almost as prominent a landmark as the cathedral. It rears up on the other side of the town square. Only the tower of it is early, but the later additions are in keeping and of the local sandstone. The records of the palace go back to a charter of 1557. The word "palace" is normal usage for a bishop's residence, but in fact this has been more of a castle than a palace, and in 1570 the men of Dornoch held it for a week against the Mackays who had seized the town. It was occupied by the earls of Sutherland, but the bishops retained the right to stay there when they toured the diocese. Originally it formed a courtyard and there are said to have been three towers.

A plaque in the cathedral commemorating the Norwegian troops who trained here during World War II calls to mind the prayer in the Litany of the Celtic Church which reads: "*A furore Normannorum libera nos Domine!*" The dreaded Northmen harried many parts of Scotland, but the great tract which is the subject of this chapter was under Norse domination for some centuries, and this set a stamp both on place-names and on the character of the people. One must distinguish, however, between good Northmen and bad ones. The bad ones were Vikings, which is simply another word for pirates. Every generation or two the fear inspired by these raiders is fanned again into faint life by discovery of another hoard of precious possessions hidden away 12 centuries ago by men and women fated never again to see what they had hidden. The National Museum of Antiquities possesses several of

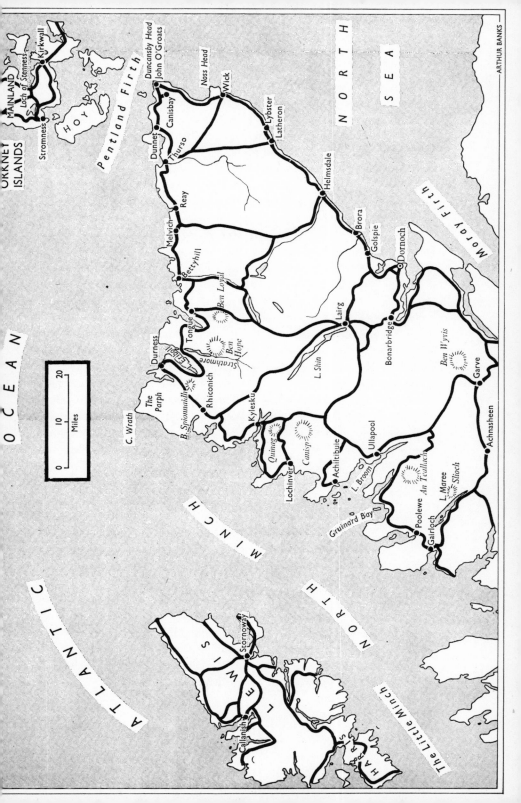

ARTHUR BANKS

these hoards: for example, the Burray and Skaill hoards from Orkney, and the wonderful Rogart or Hilton of Cadboll brooches. Rogart is only a station or two along the railway line north of Dornoch, in Strath Fleet. It is a sheltered, fertile little strath, typical of the lands settled by the Picts in these parts, and the immense concentration of brochs along this coast right up to the Pentland Firth is evidence that the north was once completely Pictish. This people was christianised at an early date. Dornoch itself was a centre of the Celtic Church. The broch pattern suggests that between Roman times and the first Viking raids in the eighth century this region may well have been as settled a community as any other of its age, tilling its fields, plying across the firths and straits with its fleets, and developing its own culture. The Vi'kingr were no ordinary invaders but hit-and-run adventurers of the most terrible kind, boatloads of men bent on orgies of rapine, men who slew and burned without mercy and disappeared into the sea-mists, their boat loaded to the strake with bullion and with women for their own pleasure or for sale to Continental procurers. They were pagans, and their paganism no doubt fed their special hatred of monastery and nunnery. The Northmen who eventually settled in the coastal parts of Caithness and Sutherland may have been more in the nature of colonists, and there must have been a good deal of intermarriage between them and the people of Pictish stock who had retreated up the glens and straths to higher ground. So the Norse names predominate on the coast—names like Brora and Helmsdale, Lybster and Wick and Thurso—while Gaelic names persist in the hinterland. Sutherland itself is simply Sudrland, the southern land.

Caithness, Sutherland, Lewis and the Orkney and Shetland islands together form a wonderful region for archaeological exploration. Relatively, at least, they look to have been more densely populated in ancient times than they are to-day. A map on which the brochs are plotted shows the coastal areas, especially in Caithness and the Orkneys and Shetlands, turned into a sort of black country, although of course those places cannot really have been densely populated. Most of the surviving brochs are not obviously recognisable as such by the un-practised eye, but there are certain outstanding examples which are impressive, even awe-inspiring, to the most casual layman. One of the more accessible is Castle Cole, in Strathbrora. Parts of it are still 15 feet high, and the site is a strong one, militarily. A better-known but more remote one is Dun Dornadilla, which rises to 24 feet and has an outer circumference of 150 feet. It is in Strathmore, close to Ben Hope, and to the road which winds from Altnaharra up to Eriboll, on the forbidding fjord of the same name, Loch Eriboll, which became known to many men of the Arctic convoys during the war. Dun is the name usually given to a broch in the Gaelic. But the most perfect of all brochs is on the island of Mousa in the Shetlands. It is 45 feet high, which is perhaps three-quarters of its original height, and it preserves better than any other the shape peculiar to the broch. Mousa itself is isolated, but there are about 75 known brochs in the Shetlands, and the usual tendency is towards fairly close grouping on good agricultural land, showing that the brochs were residences as well as forts. Many of them contained Celtic Iron Age relics.

Earlier than the brochs, and in some cases as interesting, are the stone circles, which are usually associated with the Bronze Age. The most remarkable of these is at Callanish, in Lewis, a group which includes an avenue of great stones almost 100 yards long. It is in even more wind-swept surroundings than Stonehenge, to which it comes closer in importance than any other monument of the kind in Britain. The stones of Stenness in Orkney rank almost as high. The largest of the stone circles at Stenness, known as the Ring of Brogar, covers about two and a half acres. It was the scene of a bloody battle in Norse times, recorded in the *Orkneyinga Saga*. There are a number of stone circles on the mainland, in Sutherland, for example in Strathnaver and near Bonar Bridge. But the most extraordinary prehistoric settlements in the north are located in Shetland and Orkney. All have been beautifully excavated and tidied. Jarlshof, in Shetland, explored by the late Dr. A. O. Curle, a predecessor in office of the present writer, is a Bronze Age village constructed with boulders from the beach in hollows among the sand-hills. The houses usually consisted of larger compartments with small cells opening off them. The villagers possessed sheep, cattle and ponies and grew crops of barley. Peat was the fuel used, but bronze tools and weapons were made with the use of charcoal, and the whole process of the bronze-working was revealed in detail from relics dug in the excavations. In the Orkneys are the two great sites of Maeshowe and Skara Brae. Maeshowe, by the Loch of Harray on Main Island, is

Neolithic. Indeed, it is the finest Neolithic chamber tomb in Britain, with an exterior diameter of 92 feet and an interior chamber almost 15 feet square and once 20 feet high. Some of the stone slabs forming the roof are 8 feet long. The tomb is protected by a huge ditch. Nothing was found in the chamber, which had been broken into by a band of Vikings around the twelfth century. Ironically, the desecrators scribbled some runes on the walls recording that they were Jorsalafarar, men on a pilgrimage to Jerusalem. Skara Brae is in some ways the most remarkable of the three sites, because Professor Gordon Childe was able from the objects found in the dwelling-huts and middens to build up a wonderfully detailed picture of the sort of man who inhabited this remote village. It was a primitive community, dressing in skins apparently, for nothing suggestive of weaving was discovered, and pebbles from the beach were split to serve as knives and tools were formed from the bones of the oxen, sheep and deer which they ate. The huts were linked by narrow galleries, and the middens were used to help protect the huts against the furious gales which so often strike the Orkneys, sometimes forcing people to move on all fours. Primitive as it is, Skara Brae can probably be dated to the Iron Age.

Also in Orkney, on the south road between Stromness and Kirkwall, is the remains of the only church in Scotland which can rival St. Margaret's Chapel in Edinburgh for antiquity. It is the church of Orphir, built by Earl Haakon about 1120, its circular form probably copied from some Baltic example. But not much later in date is the extraordinary cathedral of St. Magnus, in Kirkwall—extraordinary in that such a handsome, sophisticated shrine should have been built in Orkney in an age when the far north had scarcely emerged from paganism. By European standards it is modest in size, but it is beautifully proportioned and looks much larger than it is. The absence of rich carving is compensated for by the use of coloured sandstones in patterns in a way which is quite unique in Britain. The transepts, tower and parts of the nave and choir are original Norman work, but the additions made to complete it over the next three centuries in every way enhance its nobility. Both outwardly and inwardly, this is a great church. The tale of its founding is a grim one and the cathedral contains dramatic proof of its truth. The earldom of Thorfin the Mighty had been inherited by his grandsons, Magnus and Haakon. Haakon was jealous of the other's share, but the two agreed to meet to settle the matter on the island of Egilsey. Magnus came in peace, but Haakon came with eight ships manned by armed warriors. Magnus refused to involve his men in a hopeless fight, and offered to leave Orkney for ever to remain in Rome and Jerusalem, but this was rejected. Self-exile to Scotland was rejected also. Magnus then offered to be maimed and thrown into a dark dungeon, and this Haakon agreed to; but the other chiefs refused to have two earls, so Haakon ordered his banner-bearer to slay Magnus. The man angrily refused, for Magnus was a just and pious chief. Haakon commanded Lifolf, his cook, to do the deed, and Magnus himself persuaded the weeping servant. He prayed and confessed his sins, then told the other to hew him down with a mighty stroke on the head. And after, as the *Orkneyinga Saga* relates, the place where he was slain, which had been covered with moss and stones, became covered with green sward. It was the nephew and heir of St. Magnus, Rognvald III, who founded this northern church in his uncle's name. And eight centuries later, in 1926, came the sequel. The cathedral's restoration, in that year, disclosed two pinewood coffins built into the stone pillars of the choir. They contained the skeletons of two men, St. Rognvald and St. Magnus himself, and the skull of the latter was cloven by a great blow, as the Saga relates.

A perimeter drive around Caithness, Sutherland and Wester Ross is a lonely journey, but one of the most enthralling in the country. Out of Dornoch, at first it winds through rural enough surroundings, skirting Loch Fleet and running into the attractive village of Golspie. Beyond Golspie the road climbs on the shoulder of the hill country which is now always to landward, and to the south is a spacious seascape with Tarbat Ness and the Moray coast far to the south. Looking back, one is suddenly aware of the towers of Dunrobin Castle sheltering behind their woods. Dunrobin, the seat of the Duke of Sutherland, has been claimed as the oldest inhabited house in the kingdom, but in fact most of what is seen dates back no further than the mid-nineteenth century. It is an isolated mansion, and must have been more so before the present pile was built. This may perhaps have contributed to the tragic chapter in Scottish history for which, to many people, it serves as a sort of cenotaph, for the Sutherland family were absentee landlords, and in their absences crimes comparable to any deeds of oppression were committed. The original occasion of these crimes was the Napoleonic War and the need for Britain to produce more food at home. If the high, inhospitable pastures of the inland moors of Sutherland could be supplemented by the more productive land occupied by the crofters, then the quantity and quality of the sheep could be increased hugely, and this was an idea which appealed to certain factors in charge of big estates. Eviction was what they planned. For a Highland laird to evict the families on his land would, in former times, have been an unthinkable thing; but the aftermath of the 'Forty-five had broken the link between clan and chief, and surviving loyalties too often had perished through the chief's drifting away to the pleasures of the south, as on the Sutherland estates. The factors took advantage of this. Numerous crofters and small farmers were dismissed from their holdings without compensation for the crops they were losing or for the houses, which were their property. Those slow to leave had their houses fired. Sick and old were turned out of doors in foul weather and died by the score. One of the most notorious of the factors recorded in the classic *Gloomy Memories* of Donald Macleod, himself a victim, was a man of the name of Sellar, who said of one old woman too unfit to move: "Damn her, the old witch, she has lived too long; let her burn." The sheriff-substitute for the county, Robert M'Kid, reported fully on the case of Sellar, who was in fact brought to trial at Inverness in 1816; but the trial was a strange affair, one feature of which was that most of the prosecution evidence was given in the Gaelic which, Macleod records, lost much in translation, and Sellar was not only acquitted—he was complimented by the judge! As one might expect, the result was an increase in the pace of the evictions. The most convincing evidence of the tragedy to-day perhaps lies in the ruined homesteads, the heaps of stones and gaunt gable-ends, which come in sight so frequently on this wind-swept coastal road to Wick.

The coast from the neighbourhood of Wick onwards has in many places a kind of primeval barrenness. Caithness itself is a wedge of Old Red Sandstone thrust into a critical point in the ocean where the tides of the Atlantic and the North Sea meet. The seas divide on Noss and Duncansby Heads, and the scenery is such that one's awe at the strength of the waters is exceeded only by awe at the grim endurance of the cliffs. South of Wick enormous rocks, some weighing hundreds

21   *St Magnus Cathedral, Kirkwall: the South Aisle*
22–3 (overleaf)   PREHISTORIC SETTLEMENTS: *Skara Brae, Orkney* (top)
and Jarlshof, Shetland

of tons, are littered on the cliffs, and in a great storm 100 years ago waves ran up the 200-foot precipices on the west side of the isle of Stroma in the Pentland Firth and left a debris of rocks and wrecked boats on the top. The race of the tides in the Firth is powerful in itself, and when the strength of a gale is behind this the sea-passage becomes one of the most perilous in the world. This is the prospect on to which John o' Groats faces. The country about it is probably the bleakest corner of Scotland, a featureless north slope which seems to have its feet on the shores of the Arctic. But across the Firth are the weird, pale cliffs of Orkney, ghostlike on a day of haze, with the white surf reaching up them and up the pinnacle of the Old Man of Hoy in a slow motion which betrays the scale of it all. The man who gave his name to the place was a Dutchman called John de Groot, who lived about the beginning of the sixteenth century. He is not a legendary figure, and his son's tombstone is by Canisbay church, one of that small group of rather choice little immediately post-Reformation churches on which one comes with surprise and delight on this wild north coast.

A few miles west of John o' Groats the road passes through the little village of Mey. This has come into the news since Queen Elizabeth the Queen Mother purchased the old castle of Barrogill, lying about a mile to seaward of the road. This castle, otherwise known as the castle of Mey, was a Sinclair stronghold, and the Sinclairs, in spite of the unpromising bleakness of the countryside, were at one time considerable builders and patrons of the arts. A small but important token of this interest came to the Royal Scottish Museum recently by the generosity of Major and Mrs. Shaw of Tordarroch. It is a silver-mounted coconut cup, the earliest Scottish one of its kind, inscribed with the date "1588" and with coats of arms and initials which are evidently those of the Hon. George Sinclair of Mey and of his wife, Margaret. Mention of the date 1588 reminds one that some of the fugitive ships of the Armada were driven to these inhospitable seas and to those spectral cliffs beyond the Firth.

At Dunnett, overlooking a wonderful bay, is a second of those attractive little whitewashed post-Reformation churches, functionally severe yet with a simple grace acquired through a marriage of sincerity of purpose with age. Another few miles and Thurso comes in sight. Thurso is a town of much character, although it has long ago lost its

24 (overleaf)   *The standing stones of Callanish, Lewis*
25   *The mountains of Flowerdale Forest, Wester Ross*

medieval importance as the chief port for the Scandinavian trade. Its great trade in "Caithness flags", too, is not what it was, although these splendid natural flagstones of the local sandstone once bore the foot traffic of cities as far off as Paris. The flags lend a special quality even to the dykes which divide the fields in Caithness. There is little that is very old now left in the town or its neighbourhood, but the stones that are left of the bishop's palace are a reminder of the Norse rule of this region which the jarls conducted from Thurso, the name of which simply means River of Thor. The most powerful of those jarls, Harald, who died in 1190, is buried in a mound under the tower which bears his name. The Thurso of to-day has grown considerably, though in the usual graceless, mushroom fashion to accommodate workers at the atomic energy plant at Dounreay, the strange, silver-grey sphere of which looms by the sea quite appropriately in this country of queer, monolithic phenomena such as no doubt inspired the local baker, Robert Dick, to make that remarkable study of geology, the results of which have given stature to the Thurso Museum. At Reay, beyond the atomic plant, is the third and, to my mind, the most charming of the post-Reformation churches, a shapely white building by the roadside, the belfry of which has an outside stair. The date is 1739, and the laird's loft and the pulpit are contemporary, and the flags of the stone dyke by the road give just that element of contrast which the white walls need.

As soon as we cross into Sutherland the country becomes wilder and even more sparsely inhabited than in Caithness. The Caithness sandstone largely gives place to granites and schists and gneisses so occurring that the sea more and more penetrates among them in deep voes and fjords, and at the same time the country becomes hilly and craggy, culminating on the skyline in the mass of Ben Loyal. The place-names, some of them englished strangely, ring with Norse echoes, though some may be older if, for example, we accept the origin of Naver and its strath as the Nabarrus of Ptolemy. Tongue is one of the more straightforward of these names, for the Norse *tonga* means the same as the English word, and the Kyle of Tongue with its glorious golden sandy beaches is a tongue of the sea indeed. The road then makes its 10 or 12-mile detour around Loch Eriboll, with its walls of Cambrian rocks, and makes for Durness, its nearest point to Cape

Wrath. Durness is worth lingering in for two good reasons at least. The first is the cave of Smoo. This odd word seems to come from *smjuga*, a cleft. It is a double, in fact a treble cavern opening from a deep sea-cove into the soft Durness limestone, and the first chamber is more than 200 feet long. Water descends from a hole in the roof into the second chamber. Scott found this cave of romantic interest; but quite as fascinating is its significance as a limey grotto in a wilderness of sour peat, for it is this vein of sweetening rock which has transformed Durness and other pockets in the north-west. The other good reason for stopping in Durness is in the churchyard surrounding the ruins of the early seventeenth-century church. It is the monument to Rob Donn, poet of the Reay country, and one of the group of celebrated Highland bards of the eighteenth century. His was a simple, uneventful life, though he lived through the stirring time of the 'Forty-five, and it was only as a romantic onlooker that he composed songs in praise of Prince Charles and in condemnation of the Disarming Act. Most of his songs have the nostalgic, tender sorrow which the Gaelic expresses with such sensitivity, but he had both satire and a pawky wit, which came out very early in his life in a verse directed against a tailor who made him a frock buttoning behind:

> *Nay, blame not me! The tailor blame!*
> *A blundering loon was he,*
> *Who placed my buttons behind my back*
> *Where I had no eyes to see.*

The translation is Professor Blackie's. Rob Donn—Robert the Brown—had no formal education and could not read or write, but he was a cultured man, brought up to the lore of the country and also among the talk of the well-read gentry of the Mackay country. His prowess as a hunter, too, was famous, or notorious, and when his powers began to fail he is said to have climbed to the top of Beinn Spionnaidh, at the head of Loch Eriboll, and buried there among the rocks his favourite gun.

The road south from Durness is a very lonely one, with first Beinn Spionnaidh and then Foinaven on the left with the hills of the Forest of Reay beyond, and on the right the triangle of wild country known as

The Parph, reputed once to have been infested with wolves. The Parph culminates in Cape Wrath. Appropriate as Wrath seems as a name for such a stormy cape, it is simply a corruption of Parph, which is a Gaelic word related to the Norse *hvarf*, meaning a turning-point. This is indeed the point where the old seafarers turned south for the Hebrides and Ireland. At Rhiconich begins that tortuous, spectacular route between the mountains and the sea which is one of the glories of the North-west Highlands. It is so laced with lochs and fjords that often it is impossible to say whether the water one is skirting is salt or fresh, if the tide is full. The approach to the ferry at Kylescu brings into view the first of those lone mountains with strange names which make this region so different from any other part of the Highlands. It is Quinag. Quinag is a group of five peaks with cones of quartzite, its base three miles long. Canisp, a few miles further south, is another of those isolated peaks; and then come Cul Mor and, further west, on the road to Achiltibuie and the Summer Isles, Stac Polly with its fanged ridge. But the strangest of the peaks can be seen properly only by taking the side road to Lochinver at Skiag Bridge. The peak is Suilven, which means the Pillar, and a pillar it is indeed, of sandstone jutting from a bed of gneiss. It has been compared with the Dolomites, but perhaps the best comparison is with the Corcovado, the famed Sugar Loaf of Rio de Janeiro. The geological reason for those weird, isolated peaks is, of course, denudation of the sandstones by ice-masses and the peaks are relics of the vanished upper crust.

Skirting Coigach (pronounced coy-yach), the road comes down to sea and comparative civilisation at Ullapool, a beautiful village of white houses on Loch Broom. It is an eighteenth-century fishing-village and, although at close range the houses have no special architectural distinction, seen from further down the loch-side on a brilliant, windless day with reflections in the blue water the place would be hard to rival even on the Côte d'Azur or the Adriatic; for these West Highland scenes have an atmospheric subtlety difficult to find on the Continent, where everything is more obvious.

At the south end of the loch the road follows the River Broom to the Gorge of Corrieshalloch. The gorge is well screened by trees, but National Trust notice-boards advertise its presence and it is well worth investigation provided one has a head for heights. The river drops 150

26 Quinag from across the river Inver, Sutherland

feet at the Falls of Measach, contained in the gorge, and there is what seems a precarious bridge overhanging the chasm, the dramatic narrowness and verticality of which is no doubt due to its being gouged from a bed of schist instead of a softer stone.

The direct road to the east from here climbs up the Dirrie Mor to Altguish, with Ben Wyvis beyond; but to complete the circuit of the north-west one must turn west again where the roads divide at Braemore and make for Dundonnell and Little Loch Broom. This brings us face to face with what many would uphold as the grandest mountain massif in Britain: An Teallach. An Teallach (pronounced Challich) and its companions are a rugged, splintered group of peaks of the Torridonian Sandstone which predominates from Coigach down to the east end of Skye, and the north-eastern corries in particular are sculptured like monuments to the forces which wrought this part of Scotland. Once past the western buttresses, the road swings round to Gruinard Bay and the Minch comes in sight again; then, turning across a neck of land to Aultbea and Loch Ewe, we come to one of Scotland's most celebrated gardens, the National Trust property of Inverewe House. Here, sheltered from the burning, salt winds of the Atlantic by low hills and careful plantings of trees, yet so close to the water's edge that the airs of the North Atlantic Drift defeat the frosts, are palm-trees and tree-ferns and a host of other tender and even sub-tropical shrubs and plants. This Eden is, needless to say, artificial, cunningly contrived behind windbreaks patiently grown over many years, and the figure behind it is the nearly legendary one of Osgood Mackenzie, whose *A Hundred Years in the Highlands* has become a minor classic. It is precisely a century ago since Mackenzie's mother bought for him the estates of Inverewe and Kernsary, and it was upon the first of these he decided to build his home. He tells how the promontory on which he built it was largely a bare slab of Torridonian sandstone, with short heather and crowberry cover, the only soil being peat. The rest is an epic: the precarious early years of the shelter-belt, the digging of holes and filling with soil brought in creels by an old man for wellingtonias which now are grown into great trees, the bringing into the wilderness of copper beeches, chestnuts, cherries, oaks and, in time, eucalypti, cordylines, bamboos and phormiums; and ultimately the triumph of

27 *Slioch across Loch Maree, Ross and Cromarty*

showing visitors from Kew palms, loquats, Sikkim rhododendrons, leptospermums and things which grew here in the open better than they did at Kew under glass.

The road winds up over the hills and down to Gairloch, with its sheltered fishing-harbour. Here is another snug corner of the wild coast, with fine standing forests around Shieldaig Lodge and Kerrysdale, but the Falls of Kerry have been sacrificed to hydro-electric power and the beauty of the dale impaired by the pipeline. Over the next hill lies Loch Maree, in the shadow of Slioch, another of those lone Torridonian peaks. On a windless morning, with a haze on the water and nothing stirring but the duck dipping wing-tips in the mirror of the loch, the scene is like a Chinese landscape painting, and there is an eerie quality at dawn or dusk which makes the district well stocked with fireside tales even by Highland standards. Out on the loch is Isle Maree, where once St. Maelrubha is said to have had his hermit's cell, and there is a legend that two of the graves on the isle belong to a young Norse chieftain and his bride. He came back to her here from an expedition, eagerly; but she, to test his faith, came to him on her barge lying on a bier as though dead, and before she could move he plunged his dagger in his heart, and she pulled it from the wound and drove it into her own heart. And in more recent times, indeed far into the nineteenth century, the well on the isle was resorted to in attempts to cure madness. The superstitions clinging to the loch and its islands seem to have a long history going back beyond Christian times to an earlier pagan worship. By contrast, at Letterewe, on the other side of the loch, was one of the earliest, if not the earliest ironworks in Scotland. The foundry was begun there in 1607 by Sir George Hay of Megginish. One attraction was undoubtedly the thickly wooded country, necessary for the supply of charcoal, for it has been estimated that 120 acres of trees would be used annually, but as one of his partners, Lord Balmerino, had been executed for high treason the remoteness of the site may also have counted. Anyhow, according to the Letterfearn MS., Sir George "kept a colony and manufactory of Englishmen making iron and casting great guns, until the wood of it was spent and the lease of it expired". One wonders how in those roadless days the "great guns" were ever transported even as far as the nearest harbour, at Gairloch. At the lower end of the loch is the National Nature Reserve of Kinlochewe, which includes another magnificent group of Torridonian peaks: Beinn Eighe and Liathach and others. Their quartzite screes and the bare rock of their ridges and pinnacles make them more than usually spectacular, especially in spring or autumn when the snow-line is sharply emphasised.

CHAPTER TEN

Oban and the West

Oban is the natural centre for exploring the mid-Western Highlands and the Inner Hebrides. It is almost too obvious a choice, for its popularity has won it the name of the Charing Cross of the Highlands —quite unsuitably, because it is not merely a transit-point, but a very lovely place in its own right. Its man-made amenities do not match its natural ones; but even in this respect its amphitheatre of hills is given a special character by its sea-wall and harbour and by its massed hotels and even by its odd crowning feature of McCaig's Folly, looking like a sort of miniature colosseum strayed on to the heights above the Bay of Naples.

Oban itself, in spite of its bay's natural advantages as an anchorage, is largely if not entirely a product of the rise of tourism. Dr. Johnson might be called the first of its more famous tourists, for he found a reasonably comfortable lodging there in 1773, and for a long time it maintained a certain air of rather special distinction, with green and blue and ruby glasses nestling by each place on the damask-covered dining-tables in hotel windows overlooking the bay, an occasional glimpse of some such Johnsonian successor as George Bernard Shaw, and always an armada of steam-yachts, small and large, with white hulls and yellow funnels and polished brass and woodwork contemplating their own images in the ripples. For the less sophisticated there was a bus to Ganavan sands, past the ruin of Dunollie Castle.

Dunollie is a modest survival from the thirteenth century, but it was once the stronghold of a very formidable clan, the MacDougalls, Lords of Lorne. They are descended from the eldest son of Somerled, Lord of the Isles. The clan enters the recorded pages of history with the

great-grandson of Somerled, Ewen, who owed fealty for his lands both
to the King of Scotland, Alexander II, and to the King of Norway,
Haakon. Lorne in those days was on the frontier of Scotland and the
Norse domain of the Isles. A generation later the MacDougalls were
warring with the Bruce himself. It is to this time that legend attributes
the tale of the celebrated Brooch of Lorne, the proudest possession of
the MacDougall of to-day. The story goes that the Bruce found himself
in difficulties in a fight with John of Lorne and his men at Dalrigh in
Strathfillan, and that one man as he was slain clutched the Royal cloak
which, in being freed, lost the brooch which fastened it. The brooch
is said to have remained in the possession of the Lords of Lorne until
1647, when it came to the Bragleen Campbells at the sacking of Gylen
Castle on the island of Kerrera, opposite Oban, and it returned to the
MacDougalls at the beginning of the nineteenth century. It is one of a
very small group of Scottish brooches of the Renaissance period, the
dominant feature of which is a great rock-crystal, and in my view the
tradition might well be true in respect of the crystal, for such charm-
stones were greatly revered in the Highlands and were frequently
mounted in silver to mark the honour in which they were held.
Dunollie's companion castle, Dunstaffnage, was also at one time a
MacDougall stronghold, and it is well placed to command the narrows
where Loch Etive emerges into the Firth of Lorne at Connel Ferry.
Bruce drove the MacDougalls from Dunstaffnage, which became a
Campbell castle. The Stone of Destiny was said to have rested at
Dunstaffnage on its way from Ireland to Scone.

In the jewellers' shops in Oban they used to sell, and doubtless still
do sell, miniature wheel-crosses of greenstone as mantel ornaments or
pendants. Those free-standing wheel-crosses are symbols of the Irish
culture which came over with Columba in the sixth century into the
kingdom of Dalriada, and they stand for the pure Gael, with his charm
and his infuriating vagueness and elusiveness, untouched by the Norse
stiffening found further north, or by the Saxon and British elements to
east and south. Oban is the gateway to the Gaeltachd, to Gaeldom. Its
fantastic sunsets, fretted by the mountains of Mull and mirrored in the
Sound of Lorne, lend an illusion of Ossianic glories forgotten in the
soft grey drizzle of the following morning. The elusiveness one meets
with everywhere. A few years back I arrived by train with my family

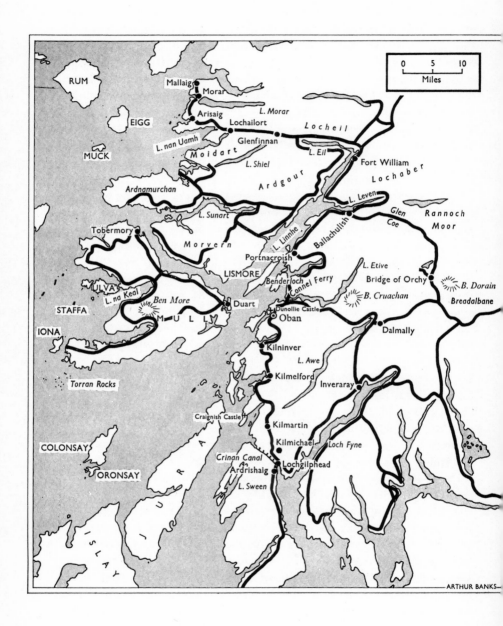

RUM

Mallaig
Morar
EIGG
Arisaig
L. Morar
Lochailort
Locheil
MUCK
L. nan Uamh
Glenfinnan
Moidart
L. Eil
L. Shiel
Fort William
Ardnamurchan
Ardgour
Lochaber
L. Leven
Tobermory
L. Sunart
Glen
Rannoch
L. Linnhe
Coe
Moor
Morvern
Ballachulish
Portnacroish
LISMORE
L. Etive
ULVA
Benderloch
Bridge of Orchy
B. Dorain
Connel Ferry
STAFFA
L. na Keal
Ben More
B. Cruachan
Breadalbane
MULL
Duart
Dunollie Castle
IONA
Oban
Dalmally
Kilninver
Torran Rocks
L. Awe
Kilmelford
Inveraray
Craignish Castle
Kilmartin
COLONSAY
Kilmichael
Loch Fyne
ORONSAY
Crinan Canal
Lochgilphead
Ardrishaig
JURA
L. Sween
ISLAY

0   5   10
Miles

ARTHUR BANKS

to join the afternoon boat for one of the Hebridean islands, to be told she was not yet in, but that she would leave at two in the morning. At one a.m. I felt my way along the sea-front in inky blackness and drench- ing rain to the pier, where the steamer was now berthed and visible in the faint glow of a brazier at which two men warmed themselves. She would, they said, be leaving at nine in the morning. Having slept in, inevitably, we came down to breakfast in the hotel at nine o'clock, in gloomy mood, and looked across the bay to watch the steamer sail. "Och, take your time now", said the soft voice of Pipe-Major Ross, here for the Argyll Gathering, "she will not be moving before eleven, whatever." And she did not.

The centre of this Gaeldom, of course, is the island of Iona, the Canterbury of the Celtic Church. It can be approached by steamer direct from Oban, or by sailing to Mull and crossing the island by a winding road to Fionphort, where a ferry boat plies across the brilliant coloured, shallow waters of a channel into which the whole swell of the Atlantic can pile at times. "Iona", beautiful name though it is, is a mistranscription. Its ancient name is Icolmkill, "Columba's isle of the church", and the church is there still, part ruined, but much of it restored very handsomely, though in the soft, moist air ferns can grow between the stones even inside the roofed church. The most beautiful of all Celtic crosses stands a few yards from the church—St. Martin's Cross, one of two or three survivors of the 360 crosses said to have been on the island at one time. There is no tortured figure on this cross, indeed no obviously didactic element at all, nor any of those naturalistic animals or humans which prance on a Pictish cross-slab. It is all a little like the soft-spoken, well-mannered postponements of the steamer-sailing, but embodied in a monolithic grandeur which well symbolises the endurance of Christianity in these storm-battered islands of the north. Small as it is, there are more kings buried here than at Westminster. There are reputed to be 48 Scottish kings, the last of them Duncan, slain by Macbeth in 1040, and tradition has it that there are also eight Norwegian, four Irish and two French kings, although their places of burial are lost. The oldest building is St. Oran's Chapel, which is a Norman building of late eleventh-century date. The remains of Columba himself were buried in the original chapel, but fear of the Norse marauders caused them to be taken to Dunkeld, and then perhaps back to the Ireland of his birth. The cathedral itself is a peculiarly beautiful building. Its coloured rubble walls, the squat pillars of the choir, the Celtic carving on the capitals, the lovely eastern windows, all these on this strange little island in high summer floating between sea and sky of such exotic hues that a whole school of Scottish painters headed by Peploe himself have devoted large parts of their lives to attempting to interpret them. The riches that once furnished cathedral, monastery and nunnery have vanished. Some handsome silver spoons dating from the early Middle Ages, dug up in the nunnery, are now in the National Museum of Antiquities. The greatest artistic glory of Iona, however, was probably its *scriptorium*, where wonderful illuminated manuscripts were produced by the monks. Some of these may conceivably be among the known Irish MSS. preserved in Swiss monasteries, notably at St. Gall, but the supreme work of the Iona *scriptorium*, as it is generally believed, is the fabulous Book of Kells which is now one of Ireland's national treasures in Dublin. The region to which Oban is the gateway in every sense spans the Irish Sea.

This link across the sea exists, strangely enough, even in geological terms. A few miles north of Iona is the island of Staffa. The meaning of the name is island of pillars, and the reason is obvious from a mile or more away, for the pastured crown of the island seems to be poised on a dense forest of cathedral columns. In fact it is a formation of hexagonal columns of a tertiary basalt, a comparatively recent volcanic rock which crops up in various places among these western islands, and which appears again on the Irish side of the water at the Giant's Causeway. Perhaps its most impressive aspect is in the various caverns which penetrate the cliffs, notably Fingal's Cave, the interior of which is cathedral-like although much of the "floor" is surging green sea. Staffa in bad weather is a fearsome place, for the waves bore into the sea caves with a boom which can be heard nearly 10 miles away on Mull, and a shepherd who once lived with his family on a hut on top of the island was so terrified by the sounds he heard that he left.

Scott wrote of Fingal's Cave in *The Lord of the Isles*, and among these islands there are many memories of the Lordship. Iona itself can show many relics in the shape of mutilated recumbent effigies of warriors and ecclesiastics buried in the precincts, but another link with the Lordship is to be found in a rather more remote and certainly

28   *Castle Stalcaire, Argyllshire*
29 (overleaf)   *From the Summit of Ben More, Mull*

much less visited spot. This is the isle of Oransay, close to Colonsay, which lies in the open sea about half-way between Mull and Jura. Colonsay is a rocky but not mountainous island, possessing some glorious beaches, especially in the sweep of Kiloran Bay from which the remote pencil of Dhu Heartach lighthouse can just be discerned on the western horizon; and in the policies of Lord and Lady Strathcona's home of Kiloran, shielded by low hills from the burning salt winds from the Atlantic, are gardens which are a paradise for peat-loving plants such as azaleas and for some of those sub-tropical things which have become acclimatised around the western coasts. Oransay is so close to the south tip of Colonsay, and the channel between is so shallow, that at low tide one used to cross in a sort of horse-drawn gig in the wake of which a seal would sometimes follow curiously. In the Middle Ages Oransay was the seat of an Augustinian priory, the ruins of which remain, and this was almost certainly preceded by a Celtic settlement, although the beautiful Celtic cross which stands there dates only from the beginning of the sixteenth century, when it was erected in memory of one Colin, prior of the community. But it is in the little prior's house which, re-roofed, looks rather like a shed, that one comes on a hoard of reminders of that strange Celtic kingdom of the west which lost its independence to the Scottish Crown only in December, 1540.

The reminders I speak of are a series of carved stones stored in the house. Some of them are effigies of knights. Some obviously commemorate ecclesiastics. The most beautiful of them, to my mind, have as their main motif simply a sword, a sword with drooping quillons, in one or two cases a portrait of the true *claidheamh-mor*, the great sword with quatrefoil terminals to its quillons, which was the supreme weapon of the Highlander down to the sixteenth century. The isolated sword is a moving symbol of knighthood. The most splendid of those sword-portraits is on a tomb-slab framed in a black-letter inscription, with the sword itself embowered in tendrils of foliage, its hilt surrounded by deer and hounds, its point resting on a galley in full sail. Now the galley is a token of the Macdonalds, the sons of Donald, the grandson of Somerled himself. They were, as Lords of the Isles, custodians of the real Gaelic tradition and culture, and their island strongholds made them difficult to reduce so that for centuries they were thorns in the

30 (overleaf) Buchaille Etive Mor, Argyllshire
31 Glencoe, Argyllshire

flesh of the kings of Scotland. What we know about the Lordship, apart
from those few, inarticulate relics, has been recorded by its enemies,
who did not hesitate to brand as traitorous any understanding between
a Lord of the Isles and an English king; and yet the Lordship was to all
intents and purposes a kingdom in its own right, with as much ground
for allying itself with England against Scotland as Scotland had to ally
itself with France against England. One cannot help a twinge of
melancholy in the prior's house on Oransay, which contains so easily
the relics of a powerful princedom between its four walls, and the
faint, eerie singing of the seals out on the skerries where their pups
blink at the pale autumn sun accentuates the odd sense of loss which so
often makes itself felt in the outer isles.

The neighbouring island of Mull was also part of the domain of the
Lords of the Isles. Their chief seat from the mid-fourteenth century
until the end of the fifteenth was at Ardtornish Castle, just opposite
Mull on the Morven coast. But the ruling clan of Mull was not the
Macdonalds but the Macleans, and Duart Castle, still the home of the
chief of the Macleans, juts like a massive sentinel from a promontory
at the entrance to the Sound of Mull. Although modified for modern
use, Duart is a magnificent example of one of the very powerful,
curtain-walled castles built to dominate a strategic point, and it seems
to grow out of the living rock. Its walls are 14 feet thick. Like many
Highland chiefs, in former times the Macleans considered they had
powers of life and death even over their wives, and the Lady's Rock,
which the steamer passes as it enters the Sound of Mull, got its name
from the act of Lachlan Mhor Maclean in exposing his possibly-
shrewish wife on the rock with the aim of allowing the tide to drown
her. She was rescued by a fisherman. She was, however, a daughter of
the head of the Campbells, the second Earl of Argyll; and when
Lachlan Mhor shortly after paid a visit to Edinburgh he was done to
death in his lodging by a relative of his wife. The Macleans forfeited
Duart for their adherence to the Stewart cause. It fell into ruin, and
remained a ruin for more than two centuries; but, like Kishmull
Castle in Barra to-day, it had the good fortune to come again into the
hands of its rightful chief, and in 1912 Macleans gathered from all over
the world for the house-warming of the restored Duart. The flag of a
chief has continued to fly over the castle ever since. The only town on

Mull is Tobermory, the Well of Mary. It is on the sheltered west side of a snug bay, protected even from the Sound by an island, and it is one of the few places on Mull which are well wooded. Its houses, reflected in the waters of the harbour, have a Continental look. To this sheltered bay in 1588 came one of the galleons of the Armada, the *Florida*, after her long, stormy passage from the Channel and round the north of Scotland. She had on board a Scots hostage, who set a light to her magazine and sank her in the bay. Inevitably, over the years the story grew that she was a treasure-ship, carrying money-chests for the pay of the fleet, and in the centuries since she sank there have been many attempts to raise her cargo, including some quite recent operations organised by the Duke of Argyll with the assistance of the Royal Navy. A variety of relics have been brought to the surface, but no treasure-chests. One of the more spectacular finds, now at Inveraray Castle, is a beautiful cannon, with the salamander and fleur-de-lis of Francis I of France, thought to have been captured from the French by the Spaniards at some such great land-battle as Pavia. Its roar was heard among the Highland hills as lately as 1854—to salute the news of the battle of the Alma! But Mull, on the whole, is a rather wild and lonely island, close though it is to the mainland. Its peaks, centred on Ben More, have none of the spectacular outlines of the Cuillin of Skye, and their slatey screes make for bleak climbing. The tremendous views, on the other hand, compensate for it: to Rhum and Eigg, to Coll and Tiree, to Colonsay and the Paps of Jura, and to all the sweep of the mainland hills with Ben Cruachan in the forefront. And at one's feet is Loch na Keal and Ulva, the first the "Loch Gyle" of Campbell's poem, the "dark and sullen water" in which Lord Ullin's daughter and her lover were lost. These hills, too, are the scene of David Balfour's weary journey after the shipwreck on the treacherous Torran Rocks, off the Ross of Mull, in *Kidnapped*. Stevenson knew this wild coast from his voyages in the *Pharos* with his lighthouse-building father.

The landward routes from Oban are fully as interesting as the seaward ones. The northgoing road by Connel Ferry skirts the great hills of Benderloch and—unlike the railway—loops round the whole length of Loch Creran and returns through the Strath of Appin to Loch Linnhe at Portnacroish. Gaeldom falls more naturally into family divisions than geographical ones—we have already touched on Macdougall country, Macdonald and Maclean—and Appin is the land of the Stewarts. The old headquarters of the Stewarts of Appin juts from a rock in Loch Laich, at Portnacroish. It is Castle Stalcaire, the Falconer's Castle, now a ruin, though enough survives to give ample material for thought. The Royal Stewart arms are still over the door to recall the sufferings of the family after Culloden. When Stewart of Ardsheal, who led the clan at the battle, was forced into exile for his part in the affair, Cumberland's men drove his wife and small children out into the snow. Indeed all Appin and its neighbourhood has bitter memories of Government treatment, memories which go back much further than the 'Forty-five and are not yet completely dead. History books for so long have been written by historians in Edinburgh or London who see the Highlands only as a perimeter area which for a time impeded the development of a united kingdom, that they have neither sympathy for nor even knowledge of the ancient bonds which were being ripped away by the central authorities in the later seventeenth and first half of the eighteenth centuries. The most notorious case of this attitude, of course, comes to mind as soon as the road swings eastward into the mouth of Loch Leven, and the grim slate-quarries of Ballachulish appear, and the grimmer entrance to Glencoe. Here, in the shadow of Buchaille Etive Mor and Bidean nam Bian, one of the most testing and dangerous mountaineering grounds in Scotland, occurred the Massacre of 13th February, 1692. The treacherous killing itself is too well known to need description; but as yet another example of the treatment which has fostered Highland bitterness and distrust, the background of the tragedy should be remembered. Macdonald of Glencoe and his sept had lived more or less as robbers and vagabonds, protected by hill and loch and the Moor of Rannoch, but now Macdonald was only too anxious to submit, like Lochiel, Glengarry, Keppoch and the others and it was in terror that he pled with the sheriff at Inveraray to accept his oath of loyalty. Unknown to Macdonald, the sheriff was not empowered to accept the oath. It was with glee that Secretary of State Stair saw his chance of revenge for the other chiefs who had escaped him by being in time. He had already written to Breadalbane asking him if he did not think this was "the proper season to maul them in the long, cold nights"; and now he gave the order "to burn their houses, seize and destroy their goods and cattle, plenishing or clothes, and cutt off the men". Ultimate responsibility for the Massacre may be laid at the door of Lochiel and others who kept the Highlands in a ferment, but the ways of the Gaeltachd were not the way of the Central Government, and it is Stair's order with the King's signature on it, and the Campbells who carried it out, that are remembered in the glen to this day.

The detour round Loch Leven is a heady tonic after the rather oppressive magnificence of Glencoe. The road climbs high along the south side of the loch, with spectacular views. Kinlochleven with its aluminium works and council houses is a jarring element in the landscape. We are not concerned with industry here, but in passing it is worth remarking that the apparently strangely situated aluminium plants here, and at Foyers and Fort William, owe their existence to water-power needed for cheap electricity for the reduction of alumina. From North Ballachulish there is a splendid road to Fort William.

Fort William, like Fort Augustus on Loch Ness, owes its presence to the constant need to check the clans. General Monk raised a fort of sorts here in 1650 as a warning to the Camerons, and in the manner of frontier forts it probably attracted a number of settlers and others who found its protecting guns useful. It is in a fine strategic position at the lower end of the Great Glen, with Loch Eil opening the way westwards and Loch Linnhe to the open sea. It has a high rainfall, surrounded as it is by high hills, including in the Ben Nevis massif the highest peak in Britain. Moreover, Ben Nevis' 4,406 feet are measured from the sea-shore which is at its base. Nevis is often spoken of as an unimpressive mountain, but only by the casual passer-by, for its northern corries and precipices are among the most fearsome in the Highlands, with what Geikie describes as ramparts of pink granite and a dark wall of porphyry, and recesses where the sun never reaches in summer and the snow never melts.

Fort William is on the threshold of the country most sacred to the Jacobites, and it is natural that its West Highland Museum should be rich in relics of the cause. Among these are many belongings and personalia, none perhaps more fascinating than the secret portrait, one of those ingenious, apparently innocent contrivances capable of revealing the most treasonable image, although of course such toys, like the Amen glasses which now fetch such formidable sums, were probably little more than playthings of sentimental old gentlemen safely recounting the bolder days of youth over the port. But only a few miles out of Fort William along what has been called the Road to the Isles are Loch Shiel and Glen Finnan, with the monument which commemorates the meeting of Prince Charles Edward with Lochiel and Keppoch and Atholl and their men and the raising of the standard of James VIII. When one stands on that spot with the tops of the hills hidden in a grey pall of cloud and a smirr of rain making leaden Loch Shiel, as on the day when the standard was raised, the tremendous personality of Charles Edward stirs one like the passing of a spirit. This is no romantic delusion. A moment's contemplation of his predicament is enough: a stranger with a few followers waiting in the rain for the coming of some disaffected chiefs he had never met with some hundreds of ragged fighting men at their backs. The man who, from this situation, could go on until he had the entire hostile country at bay had, if nothing else, a truly Churchillian doughtiness. The cause in part failed because the Highlanders, Charles Edward's main and in the end his only supporters, for all their courage and their loyalty, had their own reasons for wanting a return of the House of Stewart. Men whose ultimate aim was to bring low Argyll and his Campbells had no heart to go on from Derby, even if they had had the strength. To go on westwards along the road from Glen Finnan is to come to the place where Charles Edward set foot on the mainland of Scotland. The road emerges from the hills of Moidart, past Lochailort, and suddenly comes in view of Loch nan Uamh and the open sea. There could be no setting for the first scene of a tragedy more splendid than Loch nan Uamh, the Loch of the Caves, with its rocky headland and, floating between sea and sky, the dark patterns of Muck and Eigg and Rhum, with its great Norse-named peaks. A little further and one comes to Arisaig, with its little kirkyard where the nettles the last time I looked there had hidden another carved stone relic of the days when the Lords of the Isles ruled here, and then to the white sands of Morar, where the Atlantic rollers come in in swathes of emerald and silver and the spiked ridges of the Cuillin of Skye rise in the north-west.

The aftermath of the 'Forty-five saw a great flowering of Gaelic poetry. Rob Donn we have already met with in his country of Sutherland. The Moidart region is the scene of one of the greatest poems in the Gaelic language, *The Birlinn of Clanranald*, by Alexander Macdonald, otherwise Alasdair Mac Maighstir Alasdair. Unlike Rob Donn, he could read and write and indeed was the author of a Gaelic-English dictionary, but his Jacobitism was passionate despite the threat which hung over the Highlands after Culloden and his verses had the distinction of being burned by the common hangman in Edinburgh. But there is a special pilgrimage of an hour or two from Oban for anyone curious about Gaelic poetry. It involves following the main road east through the forbidding Pass of Brander, in the shadow of Ben Cruachan, rounding the north end of Loch Awe to Dalmally, and branching left up Glen Orchy to its end at Bridge of Orchy, behind which rises the shapely mass of Ben Dorain. The *Ode to Ben Dorain* is the masterpiece of the greatest of the Gaelic nature poets, Duncan Ban Macintyre, a traditional Highland clan bard who, illiterate, carried his entire great output of poetry in his head. He sings of the deer and of the hunting and of all the joys of existence in the glens of old, with a wealth of tender, sensitive description. Living on as he did into the nineteenth century, it was not the passing of the Stewarts that he lamented but the coming of the sheep which were to do so much more than the Disarming Acts to disrupt the Highland way of life. Duncan Ban was born close to Loch Tulla, facing the peaks of the Black Mount. He died in Edinburgh in 1812, and was buried in the churchyard of the Greyfriars there. He became a member of the City Guard in the capital, but for years after his death he was remembered as a visitor to the scenes of his youth, kilted and with a foxskin cap. The subtlety of description in his verse cannot be captured in translation, and for the English equivalent of his picture of a salmon in the eddies of a mountain stream one might do best to turn to Neil Gunn's superb passage in *Highland River*.

The route southwards out of Oban is much less well known than the routes north or westwards to the Isles. For anyone interested in the early history of the country it is a choice region, and it is of course the heart of the ancient Dalriada, first colony of the Scots from Ireland. The traditional first capital of Dalriada was Dunadd, now represented by a fortified mound close to Kilmichael Glassary in the neighbourhood of the Crinan Canal. Dunadd must have been tenanted long before Dalriada came into being, for quite a number of objects such as sandstone moulds, a stone disc and even a bone comb, belonging perhaps to the second century, have been recovered there. It was certainly occupied in the Dark Age. The first Scotic settlers from Ireland are supposed to have come around A.D. 500. It may well have been a peaceful penetration, for it is impossible now to find any distinctive cultural evidence of the newcomers. Dunadd was a strong place, a hill rising in the centre of the great moss of Crinan through which the River Add flows. It commands a wide stretch of country, including a magnificent view across the water to Jura. At its highest point there is carved on the rock a picture of a boar, and also the impression of a man's foot, this last being quite possibly a relic of the ancient custom of setting the Royal foot on the soil of a kingdom during the ceremony of crowning or appointing a new king. Dunadd remained an important place for several centuries, and it was captured at least once, by Angus, King of the Picts, in the eighth century, a few years before his final defeat of the King of Dalriada, Indrechtach, and his conquest of the Scots.

There are other ancient remains in this corner of Argyll, or associated with it. The commonness of the prefix "kil" along this road—Kilninver, Kilmelfort, Kilmichael, Kilmory—indicates the presence or former presence of a church of the Celtic period. One of the most precious things in the National Museum of Antiquities was dug out of a heap of stones at Kilmichael Glassary in 1814. It is a bell-shrine, a sort of hood of bronze made to preserve a bell held very sacred, with a crowned figure of the crucified Christ in a style characteristic of the late twelfth century and the Hand of God above with two fingers stretched downwards in benediction. It was a very moving discovery, both for its nature and for its rarity, because only one other Scottish bell-shrine is known. The enshrining of bells is itself an Irish practice, and is further evidence of the link of this part of the country with Ireland. Often the bells and their shrines had hereditary keepers. On this route, too, are two fine crosses of the sixteenth century in the Celtic tradition. The first is the Lerags Cross at Kilbride, not far from Oban, with a crucified Christ which has been compared to the figure on fourteenth-century French ivory carvings. The other, which is fragmentary, is at Kilmartin, but as a piece of sculpture it is the finer. It has all the melancholy grace of the finest medieval work.

Not very far from Crinan is the earliest surviving stone-built castle

32   *From Monument Hill, Dalmally, Argyllshire*

in Scotland. It stands on a rock jutting from the water of Loch Sween, a long arm of the sea utilised some years ago for a special experiment in the nourishment of fish by a concentration of their foodstuff. Castle Sween is a quadrangular structure with walls 40 feet high, to which towers have been added at two of the corners. It is largely ruinous to-day, with great fissures in the walls and the western sea-gate collapsed, but the entrance is in good repair and there are other early Norman features. As Mr. Stewart Cruden demonstrates, it is not, in fact, a courtyard castle, for a channel in the inner face of the curtain wall is apparently made to house roof-timbers, so that the whole thing must have been covered in. The castle was a keep, and can be ascribed to the late eleventh or early twelfth century. A Gaelic poem has survived, probably from the early fourteenth century, which describes an early naval expedition against Castle Sween (Gaelic: *Suibhne*), in which the ships are obviously the same Norse type of long galley which appears on some of the carved stones which I have described, while the warriors themselves—"golden heroes from Ireland"—seem to resemble the figures on those stones. It is fragmentary evidence of this kind which helps just a little to reconstitute in one's mind the shadowy Lordship of the Isles.

There are several other castles in this part of Argyll which should not be missed. One of these is Duntroon, on Loch Crinan, like Castle Sween well founded on a rock by the water. It is a curtain-walled castle of the first half of the thirteenth century, but it has been modernised and is occupied. Its history includes a siege by the notorious Colkitto, the great left-handed supporter of Montrose, in 1644. Then there is another objective which foiled Colkitto, Craignish Castle by the loch of the same name. And 20 miles away inland, more beautiful than the others both in setting and in itself, is Kilchurn Castle at the head of Loch Awe, in the shadow of Cruachan, in view of Inishail, Inisfraoch and Inischonel, lovely islets which stud the head of Loch Awe as the Borromean islands do the foot of Maggiore. The story goes that the keep of Kilchurn was built by the wife of Sir Colin Campbell of Lochow while her husband was crusading in the Holy Land about 1440.

33 Dunderave Castle, Argyllshire

CHAPTER ELEVEN

Inveraray
and the South-West

Although on the map it may seem fairly compact, the last area with which I have to deal is complicated and difficult of access from any one point. Although most of it is part of the mainland, it is so splintered by seaways and fjords that communications are limited largely to steamer services which are meagre as compared with the days before rationalisation set in. If I pick on Inveraray as a centre, therefore, it is in the main because it has in itself much more character than any of the comparable places.

Inveraray is one of several Scots villages deliberately created as a whole in the eighteenth century. The original village lay at the castle gates and, as fishing in Loch Fyne has usually been profitable, it may have offended ducal nostrils. The eighteenth-century village is simple, even severe in detail, but its whitewashed walls are charming in their setting of loch and hill, with the splendid woods of Duniquaich behind, and on calm days their reflections hang in the water at their feet. It is a well-planned village, the houses have naturally pleasing proportions, and those nearest the beach are linked by arches which lend a touch of character. Some of the work, including the parish church, was carried out by Robert Mylne, the architect of Blackfriars Bridge in London and of St. Cecilia's Hall in Edinburgh, a man descended from a long line of royal master-masons in Scotland. The church is a double one, the south door admitting to Gaelic and the other to English services. The mercat cross near by is an unusually fine and ancient one in the Scoto-Irish manner, and is said to be one of the crosses which left

Iona, the year of its coming being sometimes quoted as 1472. The old county buildings, now used as estate offices, are a handsome essay in classicism, and here the circuit judges at one time held court, whiling away the evenings in a hotel a short distance away in which they maintained a private cellar of excellent wines. The place has suffered a few changes. A famous beech avenue three centuries old, approached by an old gateway, was felled a few years ago, and the steeple of the church was taken down during the Second World War in the belief that passing service lorries might weaken it; but a fund has been opened for the restoration of the steeple, and a large sum of money has been spent on restorations which have brought back much of the old atmosphere. New housing near the shore has succeeded in marrying the contemporary with the traditional.

Inveraray is the capital of the Campbells. From early times it has grown under the protection of its chiefs of the Argyll family, and the Duke to this day is known to his people as MacCailean Mor, "son of the great Colin", who was Sir Colin Campbell of Lochow (Loch Awe), whose son married the sister of Robert the Bruce. The Argylls have frequently influenced the affairs of their country. Two lost their heads for their beliefs: Archibald, eighth Earl, the Covenanting leader, and his son, a follower of Montrose. They roused much hatred, however, in building up their power in Argyll, more especially among the Stewarts of Appin, and of course the Macdonalds, as recounted in the previous chapter. The bitterest wrong done by Campbells to a Stewart was done in Inveraray itself, and in the court-house. The incident is the notorious Appin Murder of 1751, used by Stevenson in *Kidnapped* and still discussed to this day. James Stewart—"James of the Glen"—had been put out of his lands by a Campbell factor, the Red Fox, Colin Campbell of Glenure, for his Jacobite sympathies, and was heard to vow revenge. Shortly after, Glenure was shot near Ballachulish. A man was seen escaping up the hill, and he was believed to be Alan Breac Stewart, whom Stevenson makes to befriend David Balfour; but Alan Breac escaped to France and James of the Glen was arrested as his accomplice. James was tried and condemned at Inveraray, on the evidence of his oath of vengeance, by a court consisting of Argyll and eleven Campbells as jurymen. Executed at Ballachulish, the hapless

James hung in chains for years at that grim spot. He could not have been guilty. Argument revolves round Alan Breac. As to the murder-weapon, I know of at least two guns which are rivals for this role, but both are army issues of a later date, although their owners or guardians are reluctant to accept this.

Inveraray Castle is an eighteenth-century building put up to designs by Roger Morris and William Adam. It replaces a fifteenth-century castle. The exterior is not beautiful, although the site is a commanding one with tremendous views down Loch Fyne, but the interior is handsome and there is a great deal of interesting material among the contents. The interior decoration is by Robert Mylne, and in general is in the style of Louis XVI, who was still on his throne when the building was completed about 1782. The north drawing-room, which is gay with tapestry panels, is the room in which Dr. Johnson was received—and in which Boswell was snubbed!—by the "beautiful Duchess". Some of the contents, for example the Teniers tapestries in the state bedroom, apparently came from the old castle, which was blown up about 1745. The spectacular display in the entrance hall is probably the chief impression of the weapons which the average visitor carries away, but I should stress that there are some fine old Highland pieces given rather less prominence, among them one of the best series of examples of the dirk in any private collection. There are, naturally, fine family portraits, by Ramsay and Raeburn among Scottish painters and also by Gainsborough and Hoppner. The cap worn by the Marquess of Argyll at his execution is shown.

Johnson, it is recorded, was highly delighted with the inn at Inveraray, rating it as good as an English one, but Robert Burns visited the place a number of years after and had a very different opinion. Burns arrived worn-out by a hard ride, but the innkeeper was busy with some gentlemen from the castle and had no time to attend to him. Burns vented his feelings by scratching them on a window pane:

> *Who'er he who sojours here,*
> *I pity much his case,*
> *Unless he's come to wait upon*
> *The Lord their god His Grace;*

34 *Inveraray, Argyllshire*

There's naething here but Highland pride,
But Highland cauld and hunger;
If Providence has sent me here,
'Twas surely in His anger.

Opposite Inveraray, on the other side of Loch Fyne, is the Cowal district of Argyllshire. Cowal is composed mostly of respectable if not spectacular hill-country, but east and south it is penetrated by fine sea-lochs for the use of which Clyde yachtsmen vie with the naval authorities. Thousands of men of more than one navy know the waters of Loch Long and Loch Striven and, of course, Holy Loch. Opposition to the basing of Polaris submarines in Holy Loch declared itself shocked at such use of the place. The popular explanation of the name is the story that a ship carrying soil from the Holy Land to put under the foundations of Glasgow Cathedral sank or went aground here; but it is more likely to have originated in the collegiate chapel at Kilmun, founded in 1442 by Sir Duncan Campbell of Lochow, some remains of which are visible near the parish church, which itself was probably built on the site of the cell of one of Columba's missionaries, St. Fintan Munnu. The Dukes of Argyll, as chiefs of the Campbells, are still buried in the crypt here. Lying among the other chiefs is the Marquess executed in 1661, whose head returned to lie beside his body after an interval of three years. The dominant Campbell note is struck again a little further up Loch Long, where the rough peaks known as Argyll's Bowling Green rise above Loch Goil. The upper reaches of Loch Long are closely hemmed in by hills ranging from 2,000 to 3,000 feet and more. At the head of the loch rears the spectacular summit of Ben Arthur, usually known as The Cobbler from its gnarled profile, with Ben Ime beyond it, and a whole ring of peaks ending in Ben Vorlich. Arrochar at the foot of The Cobbler was and still is an objective both for trippers and for the numerous serious week-end climbers from Glasgow, who find these peaks a splendid testing-ground within easy reach; but unfortunately the sheltered deep waters of the loch long ago persuaded the Admiralty to set up an establishment here, and they too have their testing-ground, for torpedo practice. The parallel though much shorter fjord of the Gare Loch has also been invaded, and to a much greater extent, by the militant outer world, although its

35 *Loch Achray and the Trossachs Hotel, Perthshire*

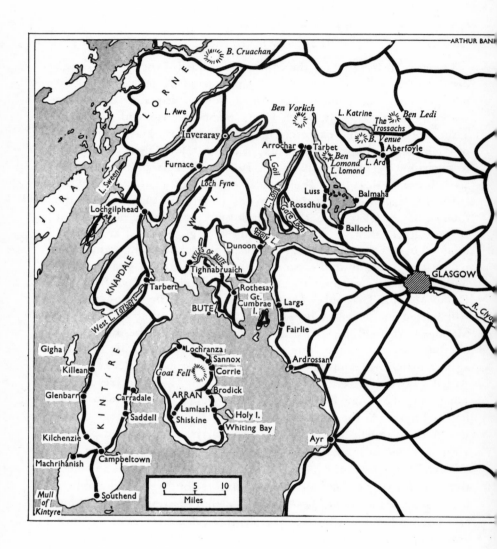

ARTHUR BANKS

B. Cruachan
LORNE
L. Awe
Ben Vorlich
L. Katrine   Ben Ledi
The
Trossachs
Inveraray
Arrochar Tarbet   B. Venue
Aberfoyle
Furnace   L. Goil   Ben
Lomond L. Ard
L. Lomond
Loch Fyne
Luss
L. Sween   Rossdhu   Balmaha
COWAL   Balloch
Lochgilphead
Dunoon
JURA   KYLES OF BUTE
KNAPDALE   Tighnabruaich
Tarbert   Rothesay
Gt.
Cumbrae   Largs
West L. Tarbert   BUTE   I.
Fairlie
GLASGOW
Gigha   Lochranza   Ardrossan   R. Clyde
Sannox
Killean   Goat Fell   Corrie
Brodick
Glenbarr   ARRAN
Carradale   Lamlash
Saddell   Shiskine   Holy I.
Kilchenzie   Whiting Bay
Ayr
Machrihanish   Campbeltown
KINTYRE
Mull   Southend
of
Kintyre   0   5   10
Miles

hills are so mild and its situation makes it so nearly a continuation of the suburban life of Glasgow, that one could almost omit it from the Highland region. Indeed, its deep-water oil-tanker berth at Faslane connects it, literally, by pipe-line, with the industrial midlands of Scotland.

Only a mile or two east of the head of Loch Long the road emerges at Tarbet on Loch Lomond. Loch Lomondside and the Trossachs between them form the best-known portion of the Highlands: indeed, for millions of people who have never set foot in Scotland, these districts are the highlands. Sir Walter, of course, is primarily responsible for this as far as the Trossachs are concerned, and one song alone must have been enough to establish the vision of Loch Lomond in the minds of strangers. The accessibility of both to Glasgow and Edinburgh has brought a formidable summer traffic of tourists, and there is no doubt that by far the best seasons to visit either are spring and autumn. At these times even the tourist-shy home Scot, who has probably seen neither since he was a child, may rediscover them for what they are— one of the choicest parts of Scotland. It is true many of their villages have been vulgarised. Camp-sites and motels and milk-bars with awful certainty have intruded upon the best views, and the roads have been invaded by every sort of terror from diesel-lorries to those young people of both sexes, on foot and pillion, who—surely as no generation before has done—set out grimly to make the least of what attractions nature has given them. But Loch Lomond and the Trossachs have just that blend of noble savagery and gentlemen's properties which appealed to nineteenth-century romantics, the sort of appeal which, at Inversnaid, moved Wordsworth to write his "Highland Girl"; and, if one closes one's eyes to the camp-sites, it must be admitted their taste was supremely civilised. Loch Lomond and the Trossachs are the Highland equivalent of the Cotswold country.

In the last chapter I compared Loch Awe with Maggiore in reverse. Loch Lomond is much nearer the mark. It comes down between the high hills in exactly the same way, and at the south end it embraces a group of choice little islets, Inchfad, Inchcruin, Inchconachan and the rest, while in tree-shaded coves lie the colourful houseboats which inspired those paintings of Leslie Hunter's, one of which the French government bought for the Luxembourg. This is perhaps merely the fringe of the Highlands adapted for Lowland convenience and pleasure, but the result—again if we except the disadvantages—is full of interest. Wordsworth and his sister did not think much of Luss, and this is not surprising as the village was so much in decay that it was about to be entirely re-housed, but Luss to-day brings to its Highland background a floral display which it would be hard to find further north. It is nevertheless Highland country, the country of the Colquhouns, the chief of whom has his seat at Rossdhu, and a century and a little more ago it was still Gaelic country, and the translator of the Bible into Gaelic, the Rev. Dr. Stuart, lies in Luss kirkyard. Like most Highland territory, the "bonny banks" were often enough the scene of bloodshed, for if the west side of the loch belonged to the Colquhouns, the east was held by the MacGregors, whose notorious temper was touched upon in the second chapter of this book. One of their bloodiest exploits took place in Glen Fruin, west of the loch, in 1603. By this time the MacGregors were desperate, for their lands had shrunk, and what they still held they held by *Coir a Claidheamh*, the right of the sword. Sir Alexander Colquhoun of Luss had been empowered by the King to put down the MacGregors who had been raiding Glenfinlas, and he had gathered a powerful force of horse and foot; but Alistair MaçGregor of Glenstrae anticipated him, and although his force was only half the size of Colquhoun's it was well handled and well armed with "halberchois, pow-aixes, twa-handit swordis, bowis and arrowis, and with hagbutis and pistoletis". He ambushed Colquhoun's men in Glen Fruin, the "Glen of Weeping", and massacred a large proportion of them and put the rest to flight, killing even some onlookers, among them a Tobias Smollett, ancestor of the novelist. The inevitable result was a fierce proscription of the MacGregors by "letters of fire and sword". The traditional burial-place of the MacGregors is on one of the islands, Inchcailleoch, the "Old Women's Island", opposite Balmaha, and Scott in *The Lady of the Lake* makes the yews which grow here the material for his fiery cross.

The fiery cross, the *Crann-Tara*, is the symbol which, from early and perhaps even pagan times, was used for urgently summoning support. Accounts of its nature vary, but according to Stewart of Garth it consisted of two sticks fixed as a cross, the cross-member being aflame at one point and the other having attached to it a bloodstained cloth.

The chief sent two men running in opposite directions with these crosses, shouting the clan slogan and naming the meeting-place, passing the cross to other runners in relay. Stewart relates that in 1745 Breadalbane sent the cross the 32 miles around Loch Tay in three hours. Strangely, the last recorded occasion on which the cross was used was in the winter of 1812–13 in Canada, when the Glengarry Highlanders were rallied to drive off an American raid.

The Trossachs is strictly the mile or two linking Loch Achray with Loch Katrine. Perhaps, however, we may make the term embrace the country all around Ben Venue, including Loch Vennachar, Aberfoyle and Loch Ard. This is the heart of Sir Walter's Highlands, and the best possible guide-books to it are the works which he wrote, especially *The Lady of the Lake*, which in 1810 began to bring here a tourist traffic which has never diminished. Sir Walter, of course, was a writer of fiction, and filled the scene with people and incidents largely invented; but the curious fact is that, the figure of Rob Roy apart, this region has little that is momentous in its history, and the best way of enjoying its beauty is to people it with the figures of Ellen Douglas and Fitz-James and Roderick Dhu. Coilantogle Ford, where the last two fought it out, has been replaced by the great sluices for Glasgow's water-supply, and the Silver Strand of Loch Katrine is hidden since the water level was raised by 17 feet, but the other old landmarks remain, and the Forestry Commission has improved some of the surrounding country by wise mixed planting. The name "Trossachs" signifies bristly or knobbly country, and the description is good, for the schistose rock has been worn into rugged outlines which, in combination with woods and water, produce a wild effect tempered by such decorative trees as oak and rowan and willow.

To return to the Clyde, the south shore of Cowal is as Highland as could be, although it is only just round the corner from Glasgow. In the absence of the holiday traffic of steamers and white-sailed yachts, Loch Striven and Loch Riddon under a darkling sky are forbidding. Even the popular resorts on the Kyles of Bute, Colintraive and Tighnabruaich, are so inaccessible by road that they might as well be situated on islands, although there is a frequent steamer service in season. On the south side of the Kyles, Bute, although far from Highland if measured by elevation, is patently part of the craggy west country. The striations which cross Scotland diagonally come down from the mountains and strike under the sea to appear again in Bute. On Bute they rear up again to 500 feet, where they emerge, ice-worn, as reefs and knobs, conglomerates resting on a mass of schist. Bute, therefore, is a part of the great Highland boundary, deep though it penetrates into the latitude of the Lowlands.

The capital of Bute is Rothesay, which is also a Royal burgh. One does not think of Rothesay in terms of history, at least of distant history, for its popularity has made it a town of hotels and boarding houses and cafés. The Glasgow family can stand on its pier an hour and a half after leaving home, even to-day. It is necessary to add the qualification "even", because in more primitive times there was a period when the journey could be done in an hour. Those were the days when 40 steamers could be seen in the Clyde at one time, when the Caledonian, the North British and the Glasgow and South-Western railways were rivals on the water and raced one another to be first at Rothesay pier. The pier is proportionately big, much larger than is usual at a Scottish resort. Many of the boarding houses used to be the rather pretentious villas of wealthy business men, and there was a time when the oldest and probably most exclusive yacht club in Scotland had its home here, but popularity has changed all this. Even so, it has escaped the vulgarity of the great English holiday meccas. The Glasgow family can still get a great deal of its amusement on the fine sands of Ettrick Bay, or messing about in a boat, and there is nothing on a small island to attract the man who is owned by his car, although it comes as a shock to read in the first published guide to the town, issued in 1855, that "cabs, minibuses and cars can be had at all times on the shortest notice"! The very core of Rothesay, however, is its castle. One prominent modern writer calls it unimpressive, overshadowed as it is in the midst of the new town, but I think that in a way the reverse is true. Its enduring mass contrasts with its commonplace neighbours, and it is one of the most interesting early castles in Scotland. It incorporates some unusual features, including a rare piece of crenellation of a battlement preserved by later heightening of the structure. But perhaps the most interesting thing about it is the light thrown on its early history by the description of its siege by the Northmen in 1230 in Haakon Haakonson's *Saga*. A scholarly reconstruction of the event has been made by Mr. Stewart Cruden. There were repeated additions to the castle, and its subsequent history reflects the commanding position of Bute, for it was occupied by the invading English, by Bruce, by Edward Baliol, and by Robert III, whose creation of the Dukedom of Rothesay for his eldest son has survived as the Scottish title of the Prince of Wales.

The family which has presided over the destinies of Bute for the past two and a half centuries is that of Crichton Stuart, the head of which is the Marquess of Bute. The home of the Marquess is Mount Stuart, a few miles south of Rothesay. The eighteenth-century mansion was destroyed in 1877, and was replaced by one which recalls the Scottish National Portrait Gallery, built by the same architect. It is magnificent in a manner which belongs to more spacious times, an extraordinary blend of Gothic towers'and marble halls, and the white marble chapel is a monument in itself. The house contains some notable art treasures, including splendid paintings and some of the most interesting silverware in Scotland. The gardens, like other more modest gardens hereabouts, reflect the benevolent effect of the mild waters of the Atlantic Drift on vegetation in sheltered places, but indeed even in the public parks of Rothesay palms grow quite happily. The genial airs and fertile soils of Bute encouraged settlements at all times in history, so that there are far more material records of man here than among all the wild hills of Cowal. They range from vitrified forts such as the one at Dunagoil, in the south, to the thirteenth-century chapel of St. Mary in Rothesay itself which, though ruined, contains the tombs of Walter, the High Steward, and Marjory Bruce, his wife, with a child. They are the ancestors of the whole Stewart line of kings.

The tail-end of the great north-east–south-west strike of the rocks of the Highlands is Knapdale and Kintyre. The diagonals are emphasised in Loch Sween and Loch Killisport and West Loch Tarbert, even in Kilbrennan Sound. This lengthy peninsula is easily accessible from Inveraray by the road which follows the upper reaches of Loch Fyne past Furnace, named from its iron-smelting days, and Lochgilphead, at the end of a shallow inlet full of sandbanks. After a few miles in the lee of the hills of Knapdale comes Tarbert, once the headquarters of the Loch Fyne fishing industry. Kintyre is rather like the abdomen of a wasp. The thin waist comes at Tarbert, where the Clyde waters of

Loch Fyne are within a mile or two of the Atlantic in West Loch
Tarbert, and Magnus Barefoot in the eleventh century, laying claim to
Kintyre as part of the island kingdom of the Northmen, had himself
dragged in his galley across the land here from sea to sea. Kintyre might
well be an island. Its obvious links with the mainland are sea-lanes, and
the circuitous land route by which most of the heavy traffic is forced
to go involves a 135-mile journey between Glasgow and Campbeltown,
eased only by the splendid engineering of the new road over Rest-and-
be-Thankful, the once formidable hill between the heads of Loch Long
and Loch Fyne. This isolation does not help Kintyre, economically
speaking, but it has perpetuated the Highland character of the villages
and countryside. Indeed, the main road down the west coast has a
Hebridean feel, with Gigha and Jura and Islay always in view, although
the wooded policies of places such as Glenbarr Abbey are more like
Perthshire. At Machrihanish the full force of the Atlantic piles up on
the spacious sands. Immense skies are reflected back in blinding light
from an immensity of tumbling waters, and this is worth a thought
because these tremendous sea-scapes were the theme of the only truly
great painter which the Highlands have produced. William McTaggart
was born near Campbeltown in 1835, the heir of a long line of small
farmers in the Laggan of Kintyre, and his grandfather's name is on a
stone in the little kirkyard of Kilkenzie, with its ruined pre-Reformation chapel and its weathered, broken monuments to forgotten chieftains. McTaggart's achievement is that in striving to capture the sparkle
of Kintyre sea-scapes in paint he devised an impressionist approach
independently of the Impressionists. The breakers and the dunes of
Machrihanish were always his favourite subject but, rather as Turner
did, he would sometimes introduce to his interpretations of light an
element of history or allegory, as in "The Sailing of the Emigrant Ship"
or the big "The Coming of St. Columba" in the National Gallery of
Scotland.

Southend, a few miles east of the Mull of Kintyre, is the spot where
Columba is supposed to have first set foot on Scottish soil. He is reputed
to have stayed here for two years before proceeding to Iona in A.D. 563.
Traditionally, the Church of Kiel, close to Southend, was founded by
him, although details of its ruins, such as the round-headed doorway,
point to a date some centuries after Columba's time. This part of

Kintyre was an obviously commanding place, viewing the whole of the western approaches to Scotland, whether to the islands or to the Clyde and the Lowlands, and the rock of Dunaverty was the site of a castle from which the Macdonalds of the Isles dominated the sea-lanes of the south-west. The castle was burned by the Earl of Sussex in 1558. It was rebuilt, but the Macdonalds were besieged in it by Argyll and Leslie with his Covenanters in 1647, and the massacre of Macdonalds which followed was one of the main charges against Argyll at his trial. It is said the Covenanters threw the defenders over the cliffs on to the rocks below, and a local writer of the mid-nineteenth century relates that he found bones and skulls at low water below what has come to be called the Rock of Blood.

The only town in Kintyre is Campbeltown, a port of about 7,000 inhabitants at the head of a small sea-loch sheltered from the east by Davaar island. Although it boasts several distilleries, there is not much of the Highland town about it. Indeed, with its air of having some industries in the background—there is a prosperous colliery—and its string of suburban villas along the shore, it is rather odd to find such a town, and a Royal burgh at that, in such a place. It is, of course, mainly a centre for the fishing fleet, and there is a tremendous influx of boats from all over Scotland when the herring brings them to these waters, but the big steam-trawlers of to-day hardly add to the amenity of the harbour as the old brown-sailed drift-net boats used to do. The ancient name of the town is Kinloch-Kerran, after St. Kieran, the missionary who preceded Columba. A cave named after him is one of several at Auchenhoan Head. There is a basin of clear water in it, and a rock with geometrical designs which might serve as a table, but the real significance of the cave is that it appears to have been a Christian chapel at one time, perhaps the earliest in Scotland. In the main street of Campbeltown stands one of the carved stone wheel crosses which one comes upon time and again in the west. It seems to date from about 1500. There are fragments of two other crosses of this period in the kirkyard at Kilkerran, on the south shore of the loch. Other places in Kintyre where such sculptured stones are to be found are Killean, Kiel and Kilkivan, the "kil" invariably signifying a church, but the largest group is among the ruins of the Abbey of Saddell, a pleasing, well-wooded village some miles up the east coast road. These are grave slabs of knightly figures, dating from the period of the Lordship, and of ecclesiastics in their robes, in the same tradition as the stones described on Iona and Oransay.

The last outlier of the Highlands with which I will deal is the island of Arran, the island which dominates the Firth of Clyde. It is so familiar to so many people in Scotland that there is a tendency to dismiss it nowadays as much less interesting than more inaccessible places, but it is in fact more interesting than most from many points of view: geological, topographical, historical. It is in the first place a most extraordinary fragment of Highland scenery to be separated only by a few miles of water from the rural Lowlands. The normal method of getting there is by boat either from Ardrossan or from Fairlie, and if the time happens to be late afternoon Arran looms up like a thunder-cloud, with avenues of sunlight striking through between the peaks to blind the eye to detail in the gloom. The big hills are concentrated in the northern part of the island, where they have weathered in the curiously varied ways of granite, ranging from the splendid cone of Goatfell (2,866 feet) to the splintered profile of the A'chir ridge. There are two good, opposed examples of the U-shaped glacial valley in Glen Rosa and Glen Sannox, where the streams have scoured the granite bottom to produce crystal pools rippled by successions of waterfalls. Round the great central nub of granite from which the peaks are carved is a belt of schists and gneisses which again vary the scenery. Then, to south and east, comes a belt of Lower Old Red Sandstone rocks, from which the material for many of the houses on the island has been quarried, and there are great outcrops of conglomerate rocks near the shore. Arran is, in fact, classic ground for the geologist, and university study parties come to it annually from as far off as Oxford and Cambridge, as they must have done ever since Bryce wrote his celebrated book more than a century ago.

Brodick, now the only port of call for the daily steamers, lies on the shore of a bay which has few rivals in this country. The slopes of Goatfell sweep gracefully down to encircle it, and there are thick woods on the north side among which the reddish pile of the castle can be seen. The castle is, since 1957, the property of the National Trust for Scotland and is therefore open to visitors. A small portion dates from the thirteenth century and contains a short staircase and a room known as Bruce's room, now used as a sort of small museum of material associated with the island. Traditionally, the Bruce watched from the battlements of the castle for the signal fire which was to be lit on the Ayrshire coast if there seemed to be hope of his return to the mainland being successful. In the sixteenth century it came into the possession of the Hamiltons, and it was as a daughter of the twelfth Duke of Hamilton that the late Duchess of Montrose had it. Its later history is in some ways more diverting than its earlier, and its innumerable visitors included the Emperor of the French, in 1847, as cousin to Princess Marie of Baden, who had become Duchess of Hamilton. Some of its annals in the nineteenth century are recorded entertainingly in *Victorian Sidelights*. Its atmosphere under the late Duchess was a delightful blend of shooting-lodge and historic mansion, and most of the beautiful contents were taken over after her death in lieu of death duties. They include some splendid silver, English and Continental. The gardens were a feature of which the Duchess was very proud, and in the shelter of the great beeches and conifers and of Goatfell itself they have become what one might almost describe as a jungle of rare things, among them an immense range of rhododendrons from all over the world.

The collection of stags' heads on the staircase in the castle is a reminder that Arran was at all times a favourite hunting domain—"Arran of the many stags", as an old Gaelic song has it. There are still great herds of deer, which come down to the shore under cover of night, and on Holy Isle there are a number of goats, although these are shy. On Holy Isle is a small cave associated with the name of St. Molios or Molaise, patron saint of the island, a follower of St. Comhgall. It was for hundreds of years a place of pilgrimage from as far away as the Outer Hebrides, and the initials of the pilgrims are the interpretation given to some marks in the cave. There is also a Runic inscription, but the belief that it refers to men slain at the battle of Largs seems unfounded. It is true enough, however, that Haakon assembled his fleet in Lamlash bay after the battle. St. Molios is reputed to have lived to 102 and to have been buried at Shiskine, the stone associated with him being carved with the figure of an ecclesiastic, but this stone does not look to be older than the later Middle Ages. There are many very old remains in Arran, a number of them in or near the pleasant, cultivated country near Shiskine, where the hedges are thick with blackberries in September. There is a considerable stone circle on Machrie Moor, or indeed a group of circles, known as the Standing Stones of Tormore. A mile or two from Tormore, in a low cliff on the shore, are some interesting caves, the largest of them known as the King's Cave because of a tradition that Bruce lived in it when he came over from Rathlin Island after the celebrated incident of the spider. Now protected by an iron grille by the Ancient Monuments Commission, the King's Cave has some early carvings on its walls. The story that these are the scribblings of Bruce and his companions whiling away the time has as much substance as the legend that the cave was once tenanted by Fingal himself; so has the attempt to connect the two-handed sword inscribed on the rock-column with the name of the Bruce, as the *claidheamh-mor* was unknown in the early fourteenth century. But the pictures of the chase have something of Pictish feeling, and may well be pre-medieval.

Even to-day, Arran bears traces of a paternalism which has done so much to shape the Highlands. The chiefs had their weaknesses like other men, and the system was fallible and in the end disintegrated. Arran, isolated by a few miles of sea, was almost a little kingdom on its own, and in recent times at least it was fortunate in those who presided over its destinies up at the Castle. There was an element of the dictatorial, on occasions, and no one could build anything on which the Castle frowned; but the island has retained a degree of independence and dignity and charm, and indeed character, qualities which have diminished in some other parts of the west and north.

Index

The numerals in **bold type** refer to the *figure numbers* of the illustrations